Step Forward
Language for Everyday Life

Workbook

SERIES DIRECTOR
Jayme Adelson-Goldstein

4 **Lise Wanage**

OXFORD
UNIVERSITY PRESS

OXFORD
UNIVERSITY PRESS

198 Madison Avenue
New York, NY 10016 USA

Great Clarendon Street, Oxford OX2 6DP UK

Oxford University Press is a department of the University of Oxford.
It furthers the University's objective of excellence in research, scholarship,
and education by publishing worldwide in

Oxford New York

Auckland Cape Town Dar es Salaam Hong Kong Karachi
Kuala Lumpur Madrid Melbourne Mexico City Nairobi
New Delhi Shanghai Taipei Toronto

With offices in

Argentina Austria Brazil Chile Czech Republic France Greece
Guatemala Hungary Italy Japan Poland Portugal Singapore
South Korea Switzerland Thailand Turkey Ukraine Vietnam

OXFORD and OXFORD ENGLISH are registered trademarks of
Oxford University Press

Executive Publisher: Janet Aitchison
Editorial Manager: Stephanie Karras
Senior Editor: Sharon Sargent
Art Director: Maj-Britt Hagsted
Art Editor: Justine Eun
Production Manager: Shanta Persaud
Production Controller: Zainaltu Jawat Ali

ISBN: 978 0 19 439235 8

Printed in China
20 19 18 17 16

Illustrations: Shawn Banner: 13, 22, 43, 55, 56, 67; John Batten: 9, 41, 70, 83;
Kathy Baxendale: 51, 71, 74; Annie Bissett: 29, 46, 72. 85; Kevin Brown/Top Dog
Studios: 24, 49, 57, 81; Bill Dickson/Contact Jupiter: 19, 31, 34; Jon Keegan: 10,
16, 45, 78; Uldis Klavins: 16, 30; Rose Lowry: 6, 22, 37, 65.

Photographs: Alamy: David R. Frazier Photolibrary, 32; Dennis Kitchen Studio:
7; Getty Images: Ron Krisel/The Image Bank, 42; Dave McNew, 11; Steven
Puetzer/Photonica, 53; Grupo Indaia: 27; NASA Kennedy Space Center (NASA
KSC): 28 (astronaut); Omni-Photo Communications: Dannielle Hayes, 2 (painter);
Photo Edit, Inc: Bill Aron, 44; David Barber, 2 (rock climber); Myrleen Ferguson
Cate, 28 (graduate); Bob Daemmrich, 4; Mary Kate Denny, 76; Tony Freeman,
21; Michael Newman, 79 (restaurant exterior); Frank Siteman, 39; Wolfgang
Spunbarg, 3; Colin Young-Wolff, 14; Punchstock: Blendimages, 79 (day care);
Photo courtesy of SMDC: 84.

This book is printed on paper from certified and well-managed sources.

I would like to thank Meg Brooks and the Oxford
editing team for their good humor, assistance and
encouragement throughout this dynamic project.

Thanks to the support of my wonderful husband and
children, I was able to fulfill my dream of writing for
ESL education.

Lise Wanage

It's been a privilege to work with Step Forward's gifted
team of editors, designers, and authors. Special thanks
to Lise Wanage—for her care and hard work, to Sharon
Sargent and Meg Brooks—for their expertise and good
humor, and to Barbara Denman—for the book without
which this book would not be.

For those who love the phrase, "Open your workbook."

Jayme Adelson-Goldstein

CONTENTS

A Write the adjectives that describe Genaro and Isabel. Use the words in the box.

~~adventurous~~	artistic	mathematical	social
verbal	quiet	athletic	musical

Genaro...

Isabel...

1. goes rock climbing. _adventurous_

2. exercises at the gym. _____

3. enjoys science and numbers. _____

4. likes parties. _____

5. draws and paints. _____

6. doesn't like noisy places. _____

7. plays the guitar. _____

8. likes to tell stories. _____

B Complete the sentences. Use the words in the box.

an auditory	a visual	a kinesthetic

1. Soo likes to read and study from her class notes.

   She is _____ learner.

2. Jose listens well in class, but he doesn't take a lot of notes.

   He is _____ learner.

3. Maria learns by doing things and using her hands.

   She is _____ learner.

A Complete the paragraph. Use the sentences in the box.

> On weekends, I play soccer and exercise.   I don't like to read auto manuals.
>
> At home, I don't watch TV very often.   I like to do activities with other students.
>
> ~~I'm an auto mechanic.~~

My Learning Style

I'm a kinesthetic learner. I learn best when I do things and work with my hands. <u>I'm an auto mechanic.</u>

                                                          1

I learn more about a car if I work with it.

_____ At school,
              2

I would rather practice than listen to a long explanation.

_____ I don't learn very well
              3

from sitting in class. _____
                                        4

I spend more time fixing things and doing yard work.

_____ I'd rather be outside than inside.
              5

B Correct the paragraph. Add capital letters and periods.

I
ɪf you know your learning style, you will be a better learner. my friend pietro is a visual learner when we are studying new words in class, pietro always asks the teacher to write them on the board he has to see the word before he can say it he also draws a lot of pictures in his vocabulary notebook he says that the pictures help him remember the new words

C Look at B. Then rewrite the paragraph.

<u>If you know your learning style, you will be a better learner.</u>

_____

_____

_____

_____

_____

A **Complete the sentences with the simple present. Use the verbs in parentheses.**

1. When Mai wants to learn something, she usually ____reads____ a book. (read)

2. When you _____ Luz something, she usually remembers it. (tell)

3. Roberto _____ around the class because he can't sit still. (move)

4. Alonzo forgets new vocabulary if he _____ the words aloud. (not say)

B **Complete the sentences with the present continuous. Use the verbs in parentheses.**

1. The students ___are preparing___ their final class project. (prepare)

2. Alonzo and Ricardo _____ a play that they wrote. (practice)

3. Luz _____ Mai about her life. (interview)

4. Roberto _____ with a partner. (not work)

5. He _____ photographs. (take)

C **Complete the paragraphs with the simple present or the present continuous. Use the verbs in parentheses.**

It's 3:30 in the afternoon at a public school in New York, and the teenagers in this picture ____are practicing____ (practice) their
$_1$
favorite "sport." Yes, these teens are on a team, but not in the usual way. At this moment, they _____ (play) chess, not
$_2$
basketball.

This organization is called Chess in the Schools. It _____ (teach) one chess
$_3$
class each week for 16 weeks. Then some students _____
$_4$
(play) chess in a chess club after school two or three times a week. In the club, students _____ (learn) from each other. One student
$_5$
says, "Right now, I _____ (work) hard, so I can play with
$_6$
students from other schools next year."

D Mark the verbs **A** (action verb) or **NA** (non-action verb).

__A__ 1. walk   ____ 5. know

____ 2. believe   ____ 6. write

____ 3. paint   ____ 7. ride

____ 4. remember   ____ 8. work

E Choose the correct verb. Circle *a* or *b*.

1. Hey! You ____ a mistake.

    a. make   (b.) are making

2. I ____ what you mean.

    a. don't know   b. 'm not knowing

3. We ____ question 2 now.

    a. 're doing   b. do

4. Oh, I ____ what you're saying.

    a. am understanding   b. understand

F **Grammar Boost** Study the Grammar note. Then circle the correct words in the conversations.

> **Grammar note: *Look/see* and *listen/hear***
>
> | **Action verbs** | **Non-action verbs** |
> |---|---|
> | *look* | *see* |
> | *listen* | *hear* |
>
> *Look/see* and *listen/hear* are pairs of action and non-action verbs. The words have similar meanings, but *look* and *listen* are more active. When you want someone to pay attention to something, you say, "Look!" or "Listen!"

1. **A:** Look! Up there! Do you ((see)/ look) that?

    B: See what? I'm (looking / seeing), but I don't see anything.

2. **A:** (Listen / Hear) for a moment! Do you (listen / hear) that?

    B: I'm (listening / hearing), but I don't (listen / hear) anything.

3. **A:** I can (see / look) it now. (See / Look)! Over there in the sky.

    B: I'm (seeing / looking)! Oh, I (see / look) it now. It's an airplane.

A Number the sentences for the conversation in the correct order.
Then use the sentences to complete the conversation.

_____ **Liang:** Well, yes, you have a point. I get nervous because the pronunciation is difficult.

__1__ **Satish:** You know, Liang, I think this class is too easy for you. Don't you agree?

_____ **Liang:** Thanks, Satish. Maybe you're right. If I practice with you first, maybe it will help.

_____ **Satish:** Oh, come on! You can speak very well. You're just shy and a little nervous.

_____ **Liang:** No, it's not that easy. The grammar is easy, but I can't speak very well.

_____ **Satish:** Yeah, pronunciation is hard. Hey, let's practice together.

Satish: You know, Liang, I think this class is too easy for you. Don't you agree?

Liang: _____

Satish: _____

Liang: _____

Satish: _____

Liang: _____

B Match the questions with the answers.

__b__ 1. Do you feel nervous in class?

_____ 2. Do you like conversation or dislike it?

_____ 3. What does *shy* mean?

_____ 4. Does he usually ask questions?

_____ 5. Does Liang think the grammar is easy or difficult?

a. No, he doesn't.

b. No, I don't.

c. He thinks it's easy.

d. I like it, but I feel shy.

e. It means to be nervous with other people.

A Read the article.

Unlock Your Memory

Use your body to build memory. Some people say that people remember 90 percent of what they do, 75 percent of what they see, and 20 percent of what they hear. Learning actively can use your whole body. You can stand up and talk aloud as you study, and use your arms, legs, eyes, ears, and voice. This puts more energy into your study time and makes it less boring.

Relax. Have you ever been unable to remember information on a test but an hour later remembered the information perfectly? This may mean that you were not relaxed during the test. Relaxation allows more blood to go to the brain and lets us think more clearly. Our brains are more awake when we are relaxed, and this helps us to perform better.

Use visualization. The more visual you can make the learning process, the easier it will be to remember the information. Create mental pictures that you can connect with the information you are trying to learn.

B Look at A. Circle *a* or *b*.

1. Some people say that _____ helps you remember more than seeing something.

   (a.) doing something

   b. hearing something

2. To put energy into your study time, the article suggests _____.

   a. sitting in a quiet place to study

   b. moving around more

3. Relaxation helps us learn because _____.

   a. the brain gets more blood

   b. we get more sleep

4. When you aren't relaxed, you _____.

   a. can't remember information

   b. can think more clearly

5. To visualize something means _____.

   a. to draw a picture on paper

   b. to picture something in your mind.

A Look at the quiz. Read the questions. Then check (✓) your answers.

Learning Styles Quiz	Yes 5 points	No 1 point	Sometimes 3 points
1. Do you understand better when you see a picture?			
2. Do you turn on the radio to listen to the news?			
3. Do dancing, sports, and games interest you?			
4. Can you easily understand maps?			
5. Do you play with things on your desk when you study?			
6. Do you remember spoken directions very easily?			
7. Do you like to eat snacks during a study period?			
8. Do you think movies are more interesting than books?			
9. Do you learn to spell by repeating the letters aloud?			

B Write your points for each question in the chart below. Add the points in each column. The column with the most points is your best learning style. Complete the sentence.

Number	VISUAL	Number	AUDITORY	Number	KINESTHETIC
1		2		3	
4		6		5	
8		9		7	
TOTAL:		TOTAL		TOTAL	

I am a/an _____ learner!

Keeping Current

LESSON 1 **Vocabulary**

A **Match the newspaper headlines with the sections or pages.**

_b_ 1. Colored Cell Phones Popular   a. front page

____ 2. Baseball's Dream Team Wins Again   b. lifestyle section

____ 3. For Sale: 2004 Toyota Pickup Red   c. sports section

____ 4. Letters to the Editor   d. editorial page

____ 5. Young Actress Wins Award   e. entertainment section

____ 6. Space Shuttle Launch Successful   f. classified ads

B **Complete the paragraph. Use the words in the box.**

top story   traffic report   ~~current events~~   headlines   weather forecast

Good evening. I'm David Lorning at Channel 14 in

Langston. Stay tuned to Channel 14 for all of the latest

news on the _____current events_____ of the day. On the

                              1

local news tonight, this is the _____:

                                      2

Volunteers in Langston are sending food and tents to the

small country of Kashman after last week's terrible earthquake.

Then our reporters, Tony Bright and Sue Marshall, will report

on the rest of today's _____: a

                                    3

woman rescued from a local river and a robbery at a Langston bank. We all want

to know when this rain is going to end, so our own Bill Jones will give this week's

_____. Then John Nolan will give us information about conditions

                4

on the roads in his _____.

                      5

A Number the sentences in the correct order. Then use the sentences to complete the story.

> _____ The robber looked at her in surprise and said, "Oh, OK."
>
> __1__ A masked man walked into the Trust Bank in Watford yesterday.
>
> _____ The police searched the neighborhood, but they didn't find the robber.
>
> _____ Ms. Martin looked at the robber and said, "No!"
>
> _____ He then turned and ran out of the bank without the money.
>
> _____ After the robber left, bank employees called the police.
>
> _____ He gave the teller, Louise Martin, a bag and told her to fill it with cash.

The Robbery That Wasn't!

_____ A masked man walked into the Trust Bank in Watford _____

yesterday. _____

_____

_____

_____

_____

_____

_____

_____

_____

_____

_____

B Look at A. Write answers to the questions. Use complete sentences.

1. What did the robber want? _He wanted money._____

2. What did the teller say? _____

3. What did employees do? _____

4. Did the police find the robber? _____

A Complete the news story with the past passive. Use the verbs in parentheses.

Red Canyon Fire Under Control

Five homes _____*were destroyed*_____ (destroy) by a
₁
fast-moving fire in the Red Canyon area yesterday. Some

people said the fire _____ (start)
₂
by campers in the area, but firefighters believe the cause

was lightning. Residents _____
₃
(tell) to leave the area Monday afternoon. No residents

_____ (injure). However, two firefighters _____
₄   ₅
(rescue) by team members following an accident. They _____ (take)
₆
by helicopter to Southside Hospital. Firefighters were finally able to control the fire by late

afternoon yesterday.

B Look at A. Circle *a* or *b*.

1. How was the Red Canyon fire started?   (a.) by lightning   b. by campers

2. How were the firefighters rescued?   a. by team members   b. by campers

3. How were firefighters taken out?   a. by ambulance   b. by helicopter

4. How was the fire controlled?   a. by a rain storm   b. by firefighters

C Write sentences with the past passive. Use a phrase with *by* + noun.

1. many homes / save / firefighters' quick response

   Many homes were saved by the firefighters' quick response.

2. other fires / start / campers in the area

   _____

3 two firefighters / injure / falling trees

   _____

4. team members / contact / cell phone

   _____

D Write *Yes/No* questions. Use the past passive and the words in parentheses.

1. Was the new hospital finished _____? (the new hospital, finish)

2. _____? (the funding for the library, approve)

3. _____? (old train station, damage)

4. _____? (the old train cars, replace)

E Complete the questions.

1. **A:** When was the new school completed _____?

   B: The new school was completed in August.

2. **A:** When _____?

   B: Construction on the new station was finished in September.

3. **A:** Where _____?

   B: The new station was built across the street from the old one.

4. **A:** Why _____?

   B: The old station was replaced because it was too small.

F **Grammar Boost**   Study the Grammar note. Then rewrite the sentences with active verbs.

Grammar note: Passive vs. active	
Passive	*Active*
The road was reopened by **the police**.	**The police** reopened the road.
Writers in English should use active verbs as much as possible.	

1. Their house was damaged by the flood.

   The flood damaged their house.

2. The new library was designed by Louisa Wright.

   _____

3. The airport improvements were approved by the city council.

   _____

4. The Red Canyon news story was written by Jeff Young.

   _____

A Complete the conversation. Use the sentences in the box.

> Maybe they can put the courts over there, far away from the building.
>
> Well, you know, teenagers need to keep themselves busy.
>
> ~~No, what's it about?~~
>
> I think I'll talk to the committee about it.
>
> No, basketball.

Ray: Hey, did you see this notice from our building association?

Jose: <u>No, what's it about?</u>
1

Ray: It says that they're building a new recreation center with basketball courts next to our apartment complex.

Jose: Did you say baseball?

Ray: _____
2

Jose: Oh no. That's going to be too noisy. Kids will play there every night.

Ray: _____
3

Jose: I can understand that, but the people here want to live in a quiet place.

Ray: _____
4

Jose: That's a good idea. _____
5

B Complete the sentences. Use reflexive pronouns.

1. They know that teenagers need to keep <u>themselves</u> busy.

2. Mr. Sato went to the meeting by _____.

3. He offered to write the report, but Ms. Moya said, "I'll write it _____."

4. We enjoyed _____ when we watched the game.

A Read the article.

On-Demand News

When people buy a newspaper or watch the news on TV, they have no control over what they read or watch unless they turn the page or turn off the TV. However, this is changing very quickly. Technology now provides more ways for people to find the news they really want—when they want it. This is often called "on-demand" news.

The Internet is the best place for on-demand news. Many newspapers and TV news programs are now making their articles and programs available on the Internet. There, people can read or view them at any time, often for free. There are also services in which a person can decide on the kind of news topics that interest them. Then stories about those topics are emailed to them. They don't even have to search the web.

The advantages[1] of on-demand news are that it saves people time and money. It also allows them to read information from various newspapers and magazines. A possible disadvantage is that people might read or view only what they want. This means that they can easily ignore[2] important national or international news. As a result, they might not know enough about these issues when, for example, they vote or make other decisions.

[1] advantage: a benefit; something that helps you
[2] ignore: not pay attention to

B Look at A. Mark the sentences T (true), F (false), or NI (no information).

__F__ 1. A newspaper is an example of an on-demand news source.

____ 2. You have to turn on the computer at a specific time to watch a news story on the Internet.

____ 3. On the Internet, you can receive only the news stories that interest you.

____ 4. Internet news is more expensive than a print newspaper.

____ 5. Most people are not interested in international news.

A Read the headline and the sentence. Underline the words and punctuation in the sentence that are not in the headline.

Headline

Town of North River Flooded After Heavy Rains

Sentence

The town of North River was flooded after heavy rains.

> **Need help?**
>
> Newspaper and magazine headlines often use a "short" form of writing. For example, they leave out forms of *be* from passive sentences and words like *the* and *a*. They also don't use end punctuation, like periods.

B Read the headlines. Then write full sentences using the past passive and *a* or *the*. Be sure to use punctuation.

Local Student Awarded Prize for Science Project

1. <u>A local student was awarded a prize for a science project.</u>

Theft Reported by North River Bank

2. _____

Local Soccer Team Defeated by Watford

3. _____

Highway 80 Closed During Hurricane

4. _____

New Bridge Opened Across North River

5. _____

UNIT **3**

Going Places

LESSON 1   **Vocabulary**

A   **Read the problems. Then choose the best advice. Circle *a* or *b*.**

1. I have a flat tire.

   (a.) Change it!   b. Send a tow truck.

2. It's dark, and my car's broken down.

   a. Turn on the hazard lights.   b. Call a locksmith.

3. I want the police to know my car's broken down.

   a. Change it!   b. Raise the hood.

4. I've tried everything. The car won't move!

   a. Get directions.   b. Put out a safety triangle and call for help.

5. I can't find Laurel Lane. I think I'm lost.

   a. Turn on the hazard lights.   b. Get directions from someone.

B   **Complete the sentences. Use the words in the box.**

out of gas   ~~locked out~~   lost   stuck in traffic

I'm _locked out_.

I'm _____.

I'm _____.

I'm _____.

A Number the sentences in the correct order. Then use the sentences to complete the story.

____ I asked her, in Spanish, about my next appointment.

____ However, I understood *las doce*. That means *twelve o'clock*.

__1__ Do you want to hear a funny language-learning story?

____ A few years ago, I was learning Spanish.

____ On Friday, when I arrived for my appointment,
I had to wait for two hours!

____ So, one day I tried to practice with my doctor's receptionist.

____ She said that it was next Friday at *las dos* (two o'clock).

What Time Was That?

Do you want to hear a funny language-learning story?

_____

_____

_____

_____

_____

_____

_____

B Rewrite the sentences as quoted speech. Add capital letters and punctuation.

1. i said i have an appointment today at twelve o'clock

   I said, "I have an appointment today at twelve o'clock."

2. the receptionist said i'm sorry your appointment isn't until two o'clock

   _____

3. i said i probably got confused about the time

   _____

4. she said i forgot to give you an appointment card

   _____

A **Read the quoted speech. Then circle the correct pronoun in the reported speech.**

1. Our friends said, "You need a new car."

   Our friends said that ((we)/ you) needed a new car.

2. My wife said, "I want a van."

   My wife said that (I / she) wanted a van.

3. The salesmen said, "We have a nice van here for only $7,000."

   The salesmen said that (they / we) had a nice van for only $7,000.

4. I said, "You have to give us a better price."

   I said that (you / they) had to give us a better price.

B **Complete the sentences with reported speech.**

1. The driver said, "The bus has a flat tire."

   The driver said that _the bus had a flat tire_____.

2. Magdalena said, "I am waiting on Cedar Street."

   Magdalena said that _____.

3. Kiana said, "I want directions to the college."

   Kiana said that _____.

4. The bus driver said, "Maple Street isn't too far away."

   The bus driver said that _____.

5. The mechanic said, "It's going to take 20 minutes to fix it."

   The mechanic said that _____.

6. Stan said, "I have to take a different bus."

   Stan said that _____.

C **Complete the sentences with *said* or *told*.**

1. Magdalena _____said_____ she had a ride.

2. The bus driver _____ Kiana how to get to the college.

3. Stan _____ he could take a different bus.

4. The mechanic _____ us the bus was easy to fix.

5. The bus driver _____ them Maple Street wasn't far.

D **Read the sentences. Rewrite them as reported speech. Use _told_.**

1. The bus driver talked to the riders. He said, "There's been an accident."

   <u>The bus driver told them (that) there had been an accident.</u>

2. Isabel said to her husband, "I'm late."

   _____

3. Ramon called Sienna. He said, "I'm stuck in traffic."

   _____

4. Rosa said to her friend, "The ambulance is coming."

   _____

E 🚀 **Grammar Boost** **Study the Grammar note. Then complete the conversation. Use reported speech in the present.**

> **Grammar note: Reported speech in present**
>
> When the reporting verb, _say_ or _tell_, is in the present, the time of the verb in reported speech doesn't change.
>
> _Molly: Hi dad. I **want** to come home from camp now._
> _Dad (to mom): Molly **says** (that) she **wants** to come home from camp now._

Al: I'm locked out of my car.

Bev: It's Al. He says <u>(that) he's locked out of his car</u>.
1

Al: I need my extra keys.

Bev: He says _____.
2

Al: The keys are in the desk.

Bev: He says _____.
3

A Complete the conversation. Use the words in the box.

> Why don't we try it?
>
> ~~If I were you, I'd take Island Road east~~.
>
> That's a good idea, ma'am.
>
> How about trying Airport Drive to Highway 24 east.
>
> I bet there won't be much traffic.

Amanda: I want to go to Red Beach, please.

Taxi Driver: Do you know the fastest way to Red Beach?

Amanda: <u>If I were you, I'd take Island Road east.</u> Then go over the bridge.
1

Taxi Driver: There's usually a lot of traffic on the bridge.

Amanda: _____
2

Taxi Driver: _____ It's longer that way, but it
3

might be faster.

Amanda: _____ It
4

will only take 20 minutes.

Taxi Driver: OK. _____
5

Please fasten your seat belt! Better safe than sorry I always say!

B **Real-life math** Complete the chart. Then answer the question.

Route	Distance (miles)	Speed limit	Time (minutes)
1. Island Road east to bridge	15	40 mph	
2. Airport Drive to Highway 24	17	60 mph	

If there's no traffic, how much time can you save on Airport Drive?

_____

(Hint: Divide the distance by the miles per hour. Then multiply by 60.)

A **Read the article.**

How to Drive Safely in the Rain

Here is some good advice about driving safely in the rain.

Keep a safe distance.
According to the National Safety Council, in normal conditions you should stay three seconds behind the car in front of you on the highway. When it's raining, you should be at least two times that distance away. A car needs much more time (and distance) to stop safely on wet roads.

Slow down.
The best way to avoid an accident during wet road conditions is to slow down. Driving more slowly allows the tires to make contact with the road. Sometimes the rain is falling very hard. When you can't see well, you are in danger. You should get off the road and park your car until the rain stops.

This car should slow down.

Avoid flooded areas.
Never try to drive across a road that is flooded by rain. You don't know how much water there really is on the road. A pool of water even one foot deep can carry a car away. Emergency workers often don't understand why drivers take risks[1] with flooded roads. When you have to drive on a wet road, drive in the middle lane. Most U.S. roads are higher in the middle.

[1] risk: a possibly dangerous action

B **Look at A. Circle a or b.**

1. When it's raining, drivers should be at least _____ the car in front of them.

   a. six seconds away from   b. one second away from

2 Drivers should _____ if they can't see the road.

   a. get off the road and park   b. stop in the middle of road

3. Emergency workers think that drivers should _____.

   a. not drive on flooded roads   b. take risks

4. The safest lane on a wet road is usually the _____.

   a. side lane   b. middle lane

A Read the scene from a TV program.

The Friday Night Mystery

Act 1

[Scene: In a darkened bedroom, Natalia is standing by the window holding the curtain back. Alexi is sitting up in bed looking confused.]

Alexi: Natalia, <u>it's 2:30 in the morning</u>. What's the matter? *[He reaches over to turn on the light.]*¹

Natalia: *[Looking out the window and motioning to Alexi with her hand]* Wait. <u>Don't turn on the light</u>. Something is happening outside.₂

Alexi: *[Gets out of bed and crosses to the window]* What's going on?

Natalia: A car is parked in front of the neighbor's house.

Alexi: <u>The neighbors are on vacation</u>.₃

Natalia: I know. It looks like two men. They're climbing over the fence.

Alexi: *[Reaching for his clothes]* <u>I'm going out there</u>.₄

Natalia: No! Don't go out! What if they're dangerous?

Alexi: <u>Then I have to call the police</u>. Where's my cell phone?₅

Natalia: It's on the night table. <u>Hurry</u>! They just broke₆ a window, and they're going into the house.

Alexi: *[Dialing]* What's the license plate of that car?

Natalia: 267-RTN.

B Look at A. Rewrite the underlined text. Use reported speech with *said* or *told*.

1. Alexi said <u>it was 2:30 in the morning.</u>

2. Natalia told Alexi _____

3. _____

4. _____

5. _____

6. _____

UNIT 4

Get the Job

LESSON 1 Vocabulary

A Complete the sentences. Use the words in the box

resource center	~~interest inventory~~	career counselor
training class	financial aid	job listings

1. "You can take an ____interest inventory____ to find a job you'll like."

2. "I need advice about my job. Can I meet with the _____?"

3. "I need money for college. How can I apply for _____?"

4. "I'm interested in learning new job skills. I'd like to take a _____."

5. "The new _____ are on the wall behind the desk."

6. "I hear you can learn a lot about different careers in this _____."

B Match the words with the definitions.

1. I don't have time to take a class outside my home. I need ____.

   a. an internship   (b.) a self-study course

2. I need some work experience, so I can get a job. I need ____.

   a. an internship   b. a vocational class

3. I'd like to learn new skills at work for the job I have now. I need ____.

   a. an online course   b. on-the-job training

A Read Joe's notes. Then complete the cover letter.

Joseph Beck
820 Porter Avenue
Lamper, MN 86352
(317)-962-2953/jbeck@wol.us
April 14, 2009

NOTES FOR COVER LETTER
Position: auto mechanic
Job Listing: in the "Lamper Times"
Experience: three years at Gary's Garage on Front Street
Training: two years, Valley Vocational College
Available: immediately

Mr. Andy Tyson, Manager
Tyson Auto Service Center
6880 Line Drive
Lamper, MN 86352

Dear Mr. Tyson:

This letter is in response to your job listing in ____the "Lamper Times"____ for the
1
position of _____. I am enclosing my resume.
2

I trained for _____ at _____. I also have
3   4
_____ of experience working at _____.
5   6
I am _____ to start work _____.
7   8

I look forward to talking with you soon. You can contact me by phone at
_____ or by email at _____.
9   10

Sincerely,

Joseph Beck
Joseph Beck

B Look at A. Circle *a* or *b*.

1. Joseph stated the job he was applying for ____.

   (a.) in the first paragraph   b. in the second paragraph

2. In the second paragraph, Joseph included information about ____.

   a. his email address   b. his training and experience

3. He did not include information about ____.

   a. how he found out about the job   b. his family and friends

A **Complete the paragraph. Use the past perfect and the verbs in parentheses.**

Mac's Moving Company needed to hire a new truck driver. After the job listing

_____had been_____ (be) in the newspaper for a week, only two applicants
            1

called about the job. The first, Soon Yung, _____ (not work) as a
                                                    2

truck driver before, but he _____ (take) a course at a truck driver
                                  3

training school. The second applicant was Arlin. He _____
                                                            4

(drive) trucks for the ABC Moving Company, but he _____
                                                            5

(have) two accidents on the job. So after the manager _____
                                                              6

(interview) the two applicants, she decided not to hire either one!

B **Combine the sentences. Use the simple past and the past perfect.**
The underlined sentence is the event that happened first.

1. Atim received her certificate. <u>She took an online course.</u>

   _Atim received her certificate_____ after _____she had taken an online course_____.

2. Atim and Malik went to the job fair. <u>They read a flyer about it.</u>

   _____ after _____.

3. <u>They filled out job applications.</u> They were called for interviews.

   After _____.

4. <u>They passed their job interviews.</u> They were both offered jobs.

   After _____.

5. <u>J. Stevens Co. hired 25 new employees.</u> Their new office opened in September.

   _____ before _____.

C Complete the questions.

1. **A:** <u>Had Omar worked with computers</u> before he got the job at the Computer Superstore?

   B: Yes, he had. He worked with computers at a college workshop last fall.

2. **A:** Why _____ before he started the job?

   B: He hadn't taken the training workshop because it cost too much money.

3. **A:** _____ before he got this one?

   B: No he hadn't. He had never had a job before this one.

4. **A:** Which manager _____ before he arrived for the interview?

   B: He had spoken to a manager named Mr. Lang.

5. **A:** How long _____ when they finally called him?

   B: He'd waited for two weeks when they finally called him.

D 🚀 Grammar Boost   Study the Grammar note. Then complete the sentences. Use *already* and the verb in parentheses.

> **Grammar Note: *Already* with the past perfect**
>
> The word *already* is often used with the past perfect. It goes between *had* and the past participle.
>
> When I arrived, the interview **had already started**.

1. When I arrived at school today, the class <u>had already finished</u>. (finish)

2. When Claudia called, the manager _____ at the store. (arrived)

3. When Camille got the job, she _____ the cashier's course. (complete)

4. When my partner came in, we _____ all the furniture in the truck. (put)

5. Xavier _____ dinner when Angie got home. (prepare)

A **Complete the conversation. Use the sentences in the box.**

> Thanks, Mr. Ellis. How about Monday?
>
> Yes, that's the one.
>
> ~~Do you mean working in a hotel?~~
>
> I took a management training class at the Jade Hotel.
>
> I'd been a cashier and an assistant manager in two restaurants.

Mr. Ellis: How are you, Ms. Yan? I'll be interviewing you for the position of hotel

manager. So, tell me, what experience have you had?

Ju-li: <u>Do you mean working in a hotel?</u>
                                                      1

Mr. Ellis: No, any experience.

Ju-li: Before I came to the United States, _____

Now I'm working at the Jade Hotel as a manager. I've been there for three years.
                                                      2

Mr. Ellis: How about management training?

Ju-li: _____
                                  3

Mr. Ellis: I've visited the Jade Hotel. Isn't that the beautiful building near J Street?

Ju-li: _____
                                  4

Mr. Ellis: Well, Ju-li, I've read your resume. You have the right skills for the job.

When can you start?

Ju-li: _____
                                  5

B **Read the paragaph. Circle the correct verbs.**

Before Ju-li ((moved) / has moved) to the United States, she
                          1

(has been / had been) a cashier and an assistant manager.
          2

Then she (found / had found) a job at the Jade Hotel. She
                          3

(worked / has worked) there for three years now. Ju-li
          4

(has finished / had finished) a management class before Mr. Ellis
              5

called her for the interview. Mr. Ellis (had read / has read)
                                                      6

Ju-li's resume before they met.

A Read the interview with singer Indaia Santos.

Indaia Santos

Q: **How did you get started as a musician?**

A: I grew up in Brazil. I was a quiet person then. I spent time alone playing my guitar every day. Later I met a poet who wanted to make his poems into music. By that time, I'd already written several songs and sung in different music groups. So, in 1994 I wrote music for 12 of his poems and made a CD of one of them. One of those songs became popular. After that, I started a band called Latin a Go Go with my husband and one of our friends.

Q: **Where has your band performed?**

A: We've performed at private parties, coffee houses, street fairs, weddings, and restaurants.

Q: **What kind of music do you play?**

A: We play salsa, mambo, and jazz. Salsa is very popular. Our music is entertaining, and you can dance to some of it.

Q: **Is it easy for a musician to earn a living this way?**

A: I have two children, so it's not easy. We work on weekends. Slowly, we have built our business, and through hard work and practice we stay busy. Did you know that some people think we play for free? People pay for jobs and services, but when it comes to artists, it's different. They think we work just for love and that we don't need money! But we do! Our equipment is expensive. We spend time practicing and getting dressed for the evening. So we have to get paid for our music.

Q: **How do people get to know about your band?**

A: People hear about us through friends. We also advertise on our website.

B Look at A. Circle *a* or *b*.

1. When she was young, Indaia _____.

   a. wrote poems

   (b.) practiced the guitar

2. When Indaia met the poet, she had already _____.

   a. written some songs

   b. written music for his poems

3. Indaia started the band _____ one of her songs became popular.

   a. after

   b. before

4. Indaia's band _____.

   a. only plays dance music

   b. plays different kinds of music

A Read the timeline. Then complete the sentences with the past perfect. Use the words in parentheses.

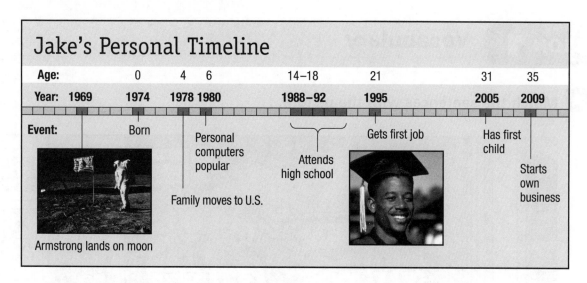

Jake's Personal Timeline

Age:	0	4	6	14–18	21	31	35
Year:	1969	1974	1978	1980	1988–92	1995	2005	2009

Event: Born — Personal computers popular — Family moves to U.S. — Attends high school — Gets first job — Has first child — Starts own business

Armstrong lands on moon

1. When Jake was born, <u>Armstrong had already landed on the moon</u>.

   (Armstrong / already / land / on moon)

2. When Jake was four years old, _____.

   (family / just / move / to the U.S.)

3. When his family moved to the U.S., _____.

   (personal computers / not become / popular)

4. When Jake was 15, _____.

   (he / already / start / high school)

5. When Jake got his first job, _____.

   (he / already /graduate / from high school)

6. When he had his first child, _____.

   (he / not / start / his own business)

B Make your own personal timeline. Follow these instructions. Use your own paper.

1. Choose at least four events from your personal life and two or more world events for your timeline.
2. Make a chart for your personal timeline with years, your age, and the events.
3. Write five or six sentences about the timeline. Use the past perfect.

Safe and Sound

Vocabulary

A Match the sentences with the picture.

_d_ 1. She's wearing gloves because the chemicals are corrosive.

____ 2. There's motor oil on the floor. It's slippery.

____ 3. He's wearing a mask. Those paint fumes are poisonous.

____ 4. The customer can't come in here. It's a restricted area.

____ 5. The office window is broken. It needs to be fixed.

____ 6. This light has a frayed cord. It needs a new one.

B Circle the correct words.

    Parking garages in shopping malls are often ((isolated) / suspicious) areas with
very few people around. (Be alert / Be active), especially in the evening. Always
stay in areas that are well lit and busy with people. (Avoid / Prevent) walking
alone in the parking lot. Have your car keys ready, and keep your eyes open.
Be aware of any suspicious (activities / accidents) around you. If you notice a
dangerous activity, (report it / prevent it) immediately.

Complete the outline. Use the words in the box.

Don't use a gas stove for heat.   Don't go outside.

Teach them to dial 911.   In case of a fire:

If you are outside: ~~Turn off electrical equipment.~~

FAMILY EMERGENCY PLAN

I. In case of a blackout:

   A. <u>Turn off electrical equipment.</u>

   B. Leave one light on to indicate when power has been turned on.

   C. _____ It can be poisonous.

   D. Keep flashlights and batteries in the kitchen.

II. _____

   A. Make sure everyone knows how to use a fire extinguisher.

   B. Make a map of the house showing evacuation routes.

   C. Make sure children know how to call for help:

      1. _____

      2. Teach them at least two phone numbers of family or friends.

III. In case of an earthquake:

   A. If you are at home:

      1. _____

      2. Stay away from mirrors and windows.

   B. _____

      1. Stay away from trees.

      2. Stand in a doorway if there's a building nearby.

A **Complete the sentences. Use *must* or *must not*.**

1. We ___must not___ go swimming now. They just put chemicals in the pool.

2. We _____ teach the children to swim. They'll be safer.

3. The pool deck is wet and slippery. You _____ run there.

4. They _____ take glass bottles near the pool. That's dangerous.

5. You _____ wear a hat. The sun is really hot.

6. The lifeguard _____ watch the children when they are in the water.

B **Write sentences with *has/have to* or *doesn't/don't have to*. Use the words in parentheses.**

1. We have a good first-aid kit. (buy another one)

   We don't have to buy another one.

2. You work with dangerous chemicals. (wear gloves)

   _____

3. She's using an iron with a frayed cord. (get a new one)

   _____

4. He has a small cut on his hand. (call 911)

   _____

5. I know exactly how to get out of the city. (use a map)

   _____

6. They heard something about tornadoes in the area. (listen for the warnings)

   _____

7. She is driving in the rain. (drive slowly)

   _____

8. He feels an earthquake. (stay inside)

   _____

C Read the list. Write sentences with *had to* (✓) or *didn't have to* (✗).

> 1. buy a new first-aid kit ✔
> 2. get batteries for the radio ✗
> 3. learn about evacuation routes ✗
> 4. bring in all the furniture from the yard ✔
> 5. put their bicycles in the garage ✔

1. They had to buy a new first-aid kit.
2. _____
3. _____
4. _____
5. _____

D **Grammar Boost** Study the Grammar note. Then rewrite the sentences. Use reported speech with *said* or *told*.

> **Grammar note: Reported speech with *must***
>
> Change *must* to *had to* in reported speech in the past.
>
> | Quoted speech | Reported speech |
> |---|---|
> | "We **must get** a new lamp." | Sven said (that) they **had to get** a new lamp. |
> | "Workers **must wear** hard hats." | He said (that) the workers **had to wear** hard hats. |

1. Karl said, "I must clean up my work area."

   Karl said (that) he had to clean up his work area.

2. The manager told Karl, "You must remove the boxes from the hallway."

   _____

3. Karl said, "I must use a ladder for that job."

   _____

4. The manager told the employees, "You must be careful with flammable liquids."

   _____

A **Complete the conversation. Use the words in the box.**

~~Now we've got a few problems~~ The streetlight is broken.
The floor is wet. We've got to fix it before dinner.
Anyway, I'll take care of it. There's a problem with the front door lock.

Myra: OK, we're finished moving in.

Now we've got a few problems.
_____
1

I'm making a list.

Emilio: OK. There seems to be a problem with the stove.

_____
2

Myra: Here's the next item.

_____
3

Emilio: You're right. You know, I tried to fix it
myself. I should have called the locksmith.

Myra: I noticed there's a leak in the bathroom.

_____
4

Emilio: Really? I hadn't noticed that.

_____
5

Myra: Do you think we should park the car on the street?

Emilio: No, I guess not. _____.
6
We should probably report it.

B **Look at A. Write sentences. Use *should have* or *shouldn't have*.**

1. Emilio tried to fix the lock himself.

He shouldn't have tried to fix the lock himself.
_____

2. The repairman didn't fix the stove.

_____

3. Myra didn't tell Emilio about the leak in the bathroom.

_____

4. Emilio parked on the street.

_____

A **Read the article. Look at the graph.**

Making Cars Safer for Children

Before the 1970s, cars were more dangerous for children than they are now. Children rode in the front or the back seat. They did not have to wear seat belts, and few people used child-safety seats. Over the last 40 years, there have been many changes that make cars safer for children.

First people realized that seat belts did not protect small children. In the 1970s, the government made TV ads announcing that children need child-safety seats. Between 1978 and 1984, all 50 states in the U.S. passed laws that required drivers to use child-safety seats. Since then, safety seats have become better. More seats are now designed to face the rear of the car to prevent babies or infants from flying forward after sudden stops.

When air bags[1] became standard in all cars during the 1990s, everyone realized that front-seat air bags were dangerous for small children. Most states have now passed laws that say children under the age of eight must ride in the back seat of the car. Although some parents still do not obey these laws, statistics show that the number who do is growing. However, many children in the four- to seven-year age group are still not riding in the back seat.

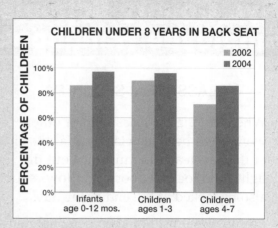

[1] air bag: a bag in a car that fills with air in an accident to protect the driver and passengers.

B **Look at A. Mark the sentences T (true), F (false), or NI (no information)**

 _F_ 1. In 1960, the law said children had to wear seat belts.

_____ 2. The government said that seat belts were better than child-safety seats.

_____ 3. By 1984, children in all 50 states had to use child-safety seats.

_____ 4. In most states, a seven-year-old child has to ride in the back seat.

_____ 5. In the 1990s, people realized air bags were not dangerous for small children.

_____ 6. Before the 1980s, child-safety seats were more expensive.

A Read the handbook.

Rye County Schools Employee Handbook

CLASSROOM SECURITY

- When leaving the classroom or other work areas between classes or at the end of the day, teachers must turn out the lights and lock all doors. Windows should also be locked at the end of the day.

- Employees must not keep personal items of value in or on their desks. Teachers should tell students not to bring valuable items to school. The district will not be responsible for the loss of, or damage to, personal property due to such causes as fire, theft, accident, or vandalism.

- All teachers have to follow these rules:

1. They must not make copies of keys.
2. They must not leave keys on desks or tables, or in mailboxes.
3. They should not give keys to students except in an emergency.

HEALTH AND SAFETY

- Staff members must report all injuries immediately to the person in charge.

- All materials that might cause someone to slip or fall should be removed from floors or other areas immediately.

- All work areas and hallways have to be free of unnecessary objects.

- Staff members must report hazardous conditions as soon as possible.

B Look at A. Complete these tasks.

1. What are two things that teachers *must not* do with keys?

   <u>make copies</u>

   _____

2. Find two sentences with *have to* and circle them.

3. What are two things that staff members must report?

   _____

   _____

4. Read the following sentences. Then write sentences with *should have* or *should not have*.

   a. Mr. Kaufman lent his keys to a student.

   _____

   b. Ms. Franklin didn't lock the window before she left the classroom.

   _____

Getting Ahead

A **Match the numbers with the parts of the conversation.**

Manager: **(1)** I thought we should have this team meeting to think of some suggestions for the problems we've had recently.

Fran: **(2)** Well, I think I should have some training to fix the new photocopier.

Manager: **(3)** Do you mean the color photocopier?

Fran: Yes, that one. The color copier wasn't working yesterday, and Kurt didn't have time to fix it. I was late with an important job.

Kurt: I see your point, Fran, but you know it's difficult to fix these machines. **(4)** You'd need a lot of training.

Fran: Yeah, I guess you're right. **(5)** I wasn't thinking about that.

Manager: OK. Here's what I think we should do. **(6)** I'm going to get another color copier. Then, if one copier isn't working, you can use the other one.

_____ give feedback   _____ ask for clarification   _____ solve a problem

_____ make a suggestion   _1_ work on a team   _____ respond to feedback

B **Circle the correct adjective.**

1. Kurt works well with many different people. He's very (responsible /(tolerant)).

2. Fran likes to learn new skills. She is (flexible / honest).

3. Fran always tells the manager if she makes a mistake. She's (honest / flexible).

4. The photocopier often breaks down. It's not very (reliable / honest).

5. Fran wants to get the work done on time. She feels (responsible / tolerant).

6. The manager knows employees sometimes make mistakes. He is (honest / tolerant).

LESSON 2 — Real-life writing

A Read the notes. Complete the memo.

Notes
Recommendation for promotion:
Moy Wong
Qualities: responsible and honest
Special training course:
Accounting Basics
Current job: mail clerk, for one year
Promotion to: accounts assistant

Memo

To: Abdul Reddy

From: Gail Evers

Re: Recommendation _____
                                                    1

I would like to recommend _____ for the
                                                                2

position of _____. Mr. Wong has worked as a
                              3

_____ in my department _____. Mr.
                4   5

Wong is a _____ employee. He is also very hardworking.
                          6

Mr. Wong has shown that he wants to learn more about the job. Last month, he

took a special training course in _____.
                                                              7

I hope you will consider Mr. Wong for this promotion.

B Write a memo. You are the supervisor. Use the information in the notes.

Notes
Recommendation for promotion:
Joena Cardenas
Current job: sales associate, six months
Promotion to:
customer service representative
Qualities: goes the extra mile;
wants to learn more
Special training course: People Skills

To: Leanne Sawyer

From: _____
                      (your name)

Re: _____

I would like to recommend Joena Cardenas for

A Underline the adjective clause in the sentences. Then complete each clause with *who, which,* or *that.*

1. Ms. Evers is a manager _____who_____ <u>respects her</u> <u>employees and tries to help them.</u>

2. These are a few of the things _____ are important to her in an employee.

3. She likes employees _____ are organized and reliable.

4. She promotes people _____ are responsible and independent.

5. At meetings, Ms. Evers makes comments _____ are helpful and not too long.

6. She knows that everyone prefers team meetings _____ are short!

B Combine the sentences. Use *who, which,* or *that* with adjective clauses.

1. Read this letter from the manager. She can solve the problem.
   <u>Read this letter from the manager who can solve the problem.</u>

2. The paychecks were in the envelope. It was in your mailbox.
   _____

3. The employees congratulated their co-worker. He was promoted to manager.
   _____

4. The company offers training courses to employees. They want to learn new skills.
   _____

5. The customer gave the feedback. It was shared with the team.
   _____

6. Abdul is the new employee. He sits next to me.
   _____

7. The manager summarized the recommendation. The employees made it.
   _____

C Read the sentences. Underline the adjective clauses. Then write answers to the questions.

1. The photocopier <u>which was installed yesterday</u> is already broken!

   What's broken? _____ the photocopier _____

2. The manager who was responsible solved the problem.

   Who solved the problem?_____

3. The Human Resources assistant who is in charge of Payroll noticed the error.

   Who noticed the error? _____

4. The team that had the best interpersonal skills won the award.

   Who won the award? _____

5. At the staff meeting which was held last Tuesday Fran made a suggestion.

   Where did Fran make a suggestion? _____

6. The employees that use the machine need to be trained.

   Who needs to be trained? _____

7. The job applicant that speaks several languages was hired for the job.

   Who was hired for the job? _____

D 🚀 **Grammar Boost**   Study the Grammar note. Match the parts of the sentences.

Grammar Note: Adjective clauses in definitions
Adjective clauses are often used in definitions.
*An **employee** is a person <u>who works for a company or another person</u>.*
*A **vocational school** is a school <u>that trains students to do specific jobs</u>.*

_b_ 1. An auto mechanic is a person   a. that students can take without a teacher.

_____ 2. A job counselor is a person   b. who fixes cars.

_____ 3. A self-study course is a course   c. that gives a student money for education.

_____ 4. A scholarship is an award   d. who gives advice about work and jobs.

_____ 5. A photocopier is a machine   e. who work from home.

_____ 6. Telecommunication workers are employees   f. that makes copies.

Everyday conversation

A Complete the conversation. Use the sentences in the box.

> Sure. Who is Cherise?   Oh, yeah, I know who you mean. Thanks.
> What should I do?   ~~Who should I see?~~

Ramiro: Hi Gerard. Do you need something?

Gerard: Uh-huh. I need the keys to the
equipment storeroom. <u>Who should I see?</u>
                                      1
Mr. Torval?

Ramiro: No, don't ask Mr. Torval. He's the owner. He doesn't
take care of little things like that. Where's Liz, your
co-worker? She had the keys this morning.

Gerard: She's on break. _____
                                      2

Ramiro: Go see Cherise. She knows where another set of keys are.

Gerard: _____
                        3

Ramiro: Cherise is the woman whose desk is near the front. She's Mr. Torval's assistant.

Gerard: _____
                        4

B Look at A. Complete the chart.

New Employee	Co-worker	Supervisor	Assistant	Owner
Gerard				

C Combine the sentences. Use *whose*.

1. Gerard is the new employee. His job is to wash cars.

   <u>Gerard is the new employee whose job is to wash cars.</u>

2. Lydia is the customer. Her car is at the car wash.

   _____

3. Mr. Torval is the owner. His assistant is Cherise.

   _____

4. Ramiro is the supervisor. His team does the most work.

   _____

A Read the article.

Dealing with Conflict at Work

If you are having a conflict with a co-worker, you should try to deal with the problem right away. Don't wait until someone gets angry. It might be helpful to discuss the problem first with someone who is not involved. For example, ask a family member or a friend outside the office for advice. This will give you some ideas about how to talk to your co-worker.

Next, try to discuss the problem with your co-worker. Be friendly, polite, and professional. Explain the problem and make some suggestions for solving it. Then ask for feedback. Listen carefully and try to understand your co-worker's ideas. Remember to be tolerant and flexible. Try to find a solution that both of you are comfortable with.

If you feel you can't talk to your co-worker, or if nothing changes after your meeting, don't give up. Talk to your supervisor. A supervisor can often explain workplace procedures. He or she should also be able to ask for changes in employee behavior without causing problems between employees.

B Look at A. Circle *a* or *b*.

1. When there's a conflict at work, you should ____.

   (a.) solve it quickly   b. get angry

2. You should talk to someone who ____.

   a. works in the same office   b. is not involved

3. When you talk to your co-worker, you should ____.

   a. be tolerant   b. demand immediate changes

4. You should work on a solution ____.

   a. that you like   b. that everyone agrees on

A Read the story.

My First Day on the Job
by Ernesto Guerra

I was very happy Lansley's Department Store had given me my first job. But by the end of the first day, I wished I had paid more attention to the 15-hour training course. First my manager, Jerry, asked me to work in the kitchen department. That was a problem because I know nothing about pots and pans, and all that stuff. My first customer was Mrs. Ramirez. She was very nice, but she had a question. So I went to ask Jerry. When I returned, there were three more customers waiting in line. The second customer, a young man named Mel Reynolds, had a credit card. Then just my luck, the credit-card machine <u>that they had given me</u> wasn't working.

By this time, another customer was getting annoyed and making comments. I started to get very nervous. Finally Sonia, a cashier who was working in the food department, hurried over to help me. She told them it was my first day. Then Jerry gave each customer a 10 percent off coupon. Suddenly, the customers changed. They told me I shouldn't feel bad at all and I was doing a great job. The customer whose name was Mr. Bernardo said, "You know, they shouldn't have left you alone on such a busy day!"

B Look at A. One adjective clause is underlined. Find two more and underline them.

C Complete the sentences. Use the names and roles in the story.

1. <u>Mrs. Ramirez</u> was the <u>customer</u> who asked the question.

2. _____ was the _____ who gave the customers coupons.

3. _____ was the young _____ who had a credit card.

4. _____ was the _____ that worked in the food department.

5. _____ was the _____ who said they shouldn't have
left Ernesto alone.

Buy Now, Pay Later

A Complete the chart. Use the words and amounts in the box. Use the
TOTALS to check your work.

savings – $3,500	~~auto insurance – $900~~	Q-card (credit card) – $2,400
income – $47,000	auto loan – $1,300	health insurance – $2,500
home loan – $105,000	home insurance – $1,400	
~~car – $6,000~~	house – $150,000	

Luis and Ximena (Personal finances)

Assets		Debts		Insurance policies	
Item	Value	Loan	Amount	Type	Premium (1 year)
car	$6,000			auto insurance	$900
TOTAL	$206,500	**TOTAL**	$108,700	**TOTAL**	$4,800

B Circle the correct words.

    Luis and Ximena wanted to buy a new car, so they reviewed
their personal finances. Their yearly ((income) / expense) from
₁
their jobs is about $47,000 a year. They also checked their
(fixed / variable) expenses, such as their utility bills and
₂
what they spend on food, travel, and entertainment. Their
(fixed / variable) expenses include the mortgage payment
₃

on their (house / car), and the (income / insurance premiums) on their house and car
₄   ₅
every year. Then Ximena said, "Let's not forget all the (fixed / miscellaneous) expenses for
                                                                ₆
different little things we buy every month." So after looking at all the numbers, Ximena and
Luis decided they should wait and buy a car next year!

A Read the outline. Then match the sentences with the paragraphs. Write *P1, P2,* or *P3.*

Topic: Borrowing and lending
Outline: Paragraph 1: Introduction. Define quotation.
Paragraph 2: Discuss problems with borrowing and lending.
Paragraph 3: Explain why borrowing and lending are sometimes necessary.

Neither a borrower, nor a lender be.

Sentences:

_P3_ Some things, like a home or a car, are very expensive.

_P2_ People often borrow too much money, and then they can't pay it back.

____ Most people could not buy these items if they didn't borrow money.

____ Borrowing and lending also creates problems between friends.

____ It means people should never borrow or lend anything.

____ People get angry if a friend doesn't return something they've borrowed.

B Look at A. Complete the essay. Use the sentences in A.
Then tell why you agree or disagree with Shakespeare's advice.

Borrowing and Lending

"Neither a borrower, nor a lender be" is famous advice.

Borrowing and lending can cause problems.

It's true that borrowing and lending can cause problems, but both are sometimes necessary.

We just have to be careful about how much we borrow or lend!

A Read the ad. Complete the paragraph. Use the present unreal conditional and the information in the ad.

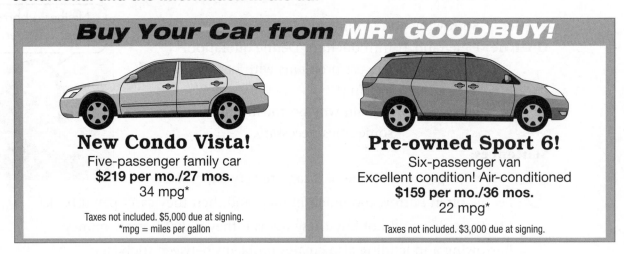

Buy Your Car from MR. GOODBUY!

New Condo Vista!
Five-passenger family car
$219 per mo./27 mos.
34 mpg*

Taxes not included. $5,000 due at signing.
*mpg = miles per gallon

Pre-owned Sport 6!
Six-passenger van
Excellent condition! Air-conditioned
$159 per mo./36 mos.
22 mpg*

Taxes not included. $3,000 due at signing.

Luis and Ximena have decided they can't buy a car now. If they

___bought___ (buy) the Condo Vista, they ___would have___ (have) to pay
  1   2

_____ a month. If they _____ (get) the Sport 6, the monthly
    3   4

payment _____ (be) just _____ a month, but they'd have to pay
          5   6

for _____ months! Also if they _____ (have) the Sport 6, they
      7   8

_____ (spend) more money for gas. They were thinking about the Vista,
  9

but the small print said they had to pay _____ when they signed the
                                            10

contract! Ximena said, "We always read the small print. If we _____ (not
                                                                11

do) that, we _____ (be) in trouble!"
               12

B Combine the sentences. Use the present unreal conditional.

1. I don't have enough money. I won't buy that blue car.

   If I had _enough money, I would buy that blue car_____.

2. We don't have car insurance. I can't drive the car.

   If we had _____.

3. We save money every month. We can take a vacation every year.

   But, if we didn't _____.

4. He pays the bills on time. He doesn't have to pay late fees.

   If he didn't _____.

C Complete the questions and answers. Use the present unreal conditional and the verbs in parentheses.

1. **A:** If Gary _____had_____ enough money, would he _____go_____ to college? (have, go)

   B: Yes, he _____would_____. He wants to go.

2. **A:** How much _____ it _____ if he _____ to a community college? (cost, go)

   B: It _____ more than $5,000. (cost)

3. **A:** _____ he _____ in school if he _____ a part-time job? (stay, find)

   B: Yes, I think he _____.

4. **A:** If he _____, _____ he _____ better grades? (not work, get)

   B: Probably. He _____ more time to study. (have)

5. **A:** If we _____ him, _____ he _____ hard? (help, work)

   B: Of course, he _____.

D 🚀 **Grammar Boost** Study the Grammar note. Then complete the conversation with real or unreal conditionals. Use the verbs in parentheses.

Grammar note: Real vs. present unreal conditionals

Real conditionals . . .	*Unreal conditionals . . .*
• use the present in the *if* clause.	• use the past in the *if* clause.
• use *will* in the main clause.	• use *would* in the main clause.
If I go on the trip, I'll enjoy it.	*If I went on the trip, I'd enjoy it.*

Terry: If I decide to buy a house, I'll try _____ to get a bank loan. (try)
                                    1

Pat: If you apply for a loan, you _____ a few weeks. (have to wait)
                                    2

Terry: I'll be lucky if I _____ a house in a good neighborhood. (find)
                          3

Pat: Hmm. If you bought an old house and fixed it up, it _____ cheaper. (be)
                                                          4

Terry: Yes, it would be cheaper if I _____ the work myself. (do)
                                       5

Pat: If you had to pay people to do the work, it _____ too expensive. (be)
                                                  6

Terry: If I were a millionaire, I _____ so much! (have to worry)
                                   7

A Complete the conversation. Use the sentences in the box.

> How about if we go on Monday afternoon?   Business Mart is 30 miles away.
>
> Well, what if we shop there once a month?   When do you want to go?
>
> ~~You know, we shouldn't buy so much there.~~

Jon: We need a few things for the coffee shop. I think I'll go to that store on the corner.

Yen: <u>You know, we shouldn't buy so much there.</u> It's expensive.
                          1

Jon: If I went to Business Mart, we'd save money.

Yen: _____ You don't have time to drive that far
                      2

every week.

Jon: _____ We could buy most of our supplies there.
                      3

Yen: That's a good idea. _____
                                        4

Jon: _____
                      5

Yen: OK. The shop isn't very busy on Mondays.

B Look at A. Combine the sentences. Use the unreal conditional with *be*.

1. The prices are too high. Jon and Yen won't shop at the local store.

   <u>If the prices weren't too high, Jon and Yen would shop at the local store.</u>

2. Business Mart is so far away. They won't drive there every week.

   _____

3. Jon will buy most of their supplies at Business Mart. He will save money there.

   _____

4. The coffee shop isn't busy on Mondays. They will have time to go shopping.

   _____

C **Real-life math** Read about Jon and Yen's business. Circle *a, b,* or *c*.

Jon and Yen now spend about $150.00 a week on supplies like napkins, paper towels, and cups, for the coffee shop. If they did all their shopping at Business Mart, they would save about $22.50 a week.

In four weeks, they would save about _____.

a. $150   b. $50   c. $90

A Read the article.

Money Manners

Different cultures often have different ideas about what is polite when talking about money. In the U.S., for example, people often consider income and financial topics to be private. It is not considered good manners to ask a direct question about someone's salary. Even good friends often do not share this information with each other. In the workplace, you should only discuss your salary with your supervisor. Many companies protect employee salary information.

Wow! This is nice stuff. How much did it cost?

Also, it is best not to ask what things cost. For example, when visiting someone's home, it is fine to say that you like their furniture or something they are wearing. However, it is not a good idea to ask how much these things cost. This is especially true of expensive items such as a car or a house.

If someone asks you about your income, you don't have to answer the question. For example, you could say with a smile something like, "If I told you, you'd be surprised" or "I'd really rather not say." If you really needed to know how much someone paid for a small item, you could say, "Excuse me, but would you mind telling me how much that cost? I'll understand if you don't want to tell me."

B Look at A. Mark the statements and questions as Appropriate (A) or Not Appropriate (NA) in a social conversation

_NA_ 1. Hi, Joe. Tell me, how much is the company paying you these days?

_____ 2. Wow! I like this TV. The picture's really clear.

_____ 3. Great house, Mary! How much did you pay for it?

_____ 4. I'd really rather not talk about my salary right now.

_____ 5. This is a nice cell phone. Would you mind if I asked how much it cost?

Complete the sentences. Use the present unreal conditional and your own ideas.

If I . . .

If I had more time on the weekend, I would go for a walk on the beach.

1. If I had more time on the weekend,

   I _____.

2. If I were in the supermarket and saw someone stealing food,

   I _____.

3. If I could be anything I wanted to,

   I _____.

4. If I found $100 on a bus,

   I _____.

5. If I had time to take another class,

   I _____.

6. If I ever had the courage,

   I _____.

7. If I had the chance to visit any country in the world,

   I _____.

8. If I designed my own house,

   it _____.

9. If I were able to _____

   I _____.

10. If I had a chance to meet someone famous,

    I _____.

11. If I lived near _____

    I _____.

12. If I had the chance to change one thing in my life,

    I _____.

Satisfaction Guaranteed

LESSON 1 **Vocabulary**

A **Circle the correct words.**

Rosa: What is all this, Viki? Are you having a ((yard sale) / thrift store) today?

1

Viki: Uh-huh. Remember this old chair? We bought it at the Saturday

(thrift store / flea market) downtown.

2

Rosa: Yeah, we had a good time that day. Why are you selling this beautiful table?

Oh, I see. It's scratched.

Viki: It was always scratched. I bought it (as is / online) from that discount furniture

3

store for $25.

Rosa: Do you want to go to the sale at Markham's Jewelry store tomorrow? Everything is

(as is / on clearance).

4

Viki: No thanks. I don't like crowds. It's easier to use my computer to shop the

(online stores / yard sales).

5

B **Write the correct words under the pictures. Use the words in the box.**

| stained | dented | torn | ~~scratched~~ | faded | defective |

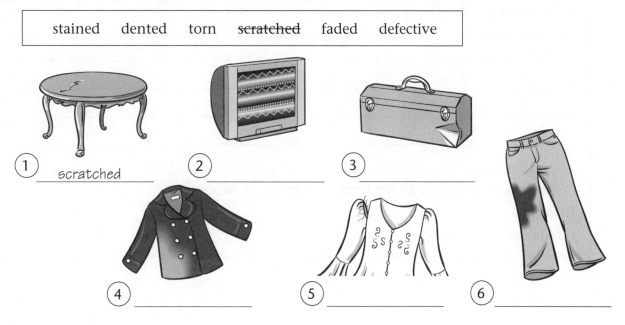

1. _____scratched_____

2. _____

3. _____

4. _____

5. _____

6. _____

A **Read the outline. Then match the sentences with the paragraphs.**
Write *P1, P2,* or *P3.*

Topic: Order problem with CameraLand

Outline: Paragraph 1: Say where and when video camera was bought.
Say there's a problem.
Paragraph 2: Explain the problem.
Paragraph 3: Say what you want the company to do.

Sentences:

_P2_ First, the camera is defective. It doesn't rewind.

_P1_ I ordered a Sanvey 200 video camera from your online store on March 2.

_____ If you cannot fix the camera, please send me a new one.

_____ I received the camera on March 20, but there are some problems with
the order.

_____ Second, the price of the camera was $299.00, but on the bill I was charged
$350.00.

_____ Finally, I would also like a new bill for the correct amount.

B **Complete the email to CameraLand. Use the sentences in A.**

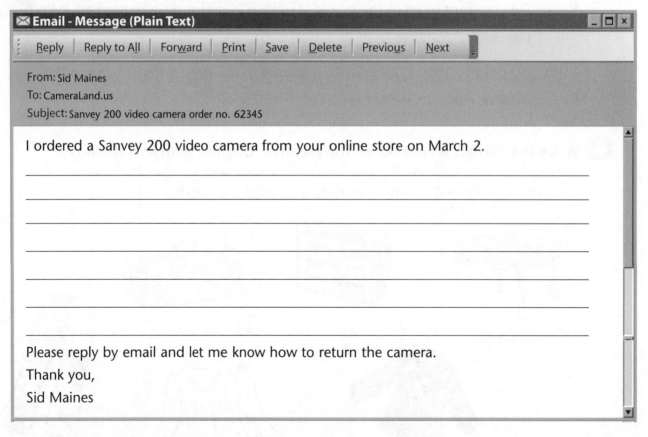

Email - Message (Plain Text)

Reply | Reply to All | Forward | Print | Save | Delete | Previous | Next

From: Sid Maines
To: CameraLand.us
Subject: Sanvey 200 video camera order no. 62345

I ordered a Sanvey 200 video camera from your online store on March 2.

_____

_____

_____

_____

_____

_____

_____

Please reply by email and let me know how to return the camera.

Thank you,

Sid Maines

A **Complete the sentences. Use the -ing or the -ed form of the adjectives in parentheses.**

1. We were ___surprised___ when our cousin invited us to go shopping in the city. (surprise)

2. When we arrived, she was _____ to see us. (excite)

3. Everyone was _____ about where to go, but we finally found some good stores. (confuse)

4. We had an _____ time shopping at a flea market. (interest)

5. On the last day, the weather was _____. It started raining. (disappoint)

6. I had a great time. It's never _____ downtown in the big city! (bore)

B **Complete sentences with the -ed or -ing form of the underlined verb.**

1. The first view of the island <u>excited</u> everyone.

   a. The first view of the island was ___exciting___.

   b. Everyone was ___excited___.

2. But the shopping trip <u>disappointed</u> the tourists.

   a. The shopping trip was _____.

   b. The tourists were _____.

3. The prices <u>surprised</u> them.

   a. They were _____.

   b. The prices were _____.

4. The stores didn't <u>interest</u> us.

   a. The shops weren't _____.

   b. We weren't _____.

5. The directions <u>confused</u> him.

   a. He was _____.

   b. The directions were _____.

C Circle the correct adjectives.

Eric was (boring /(bored)) with his usual everyday schedule. He wanted to have

an (excited / exciting) weekend. He wasn't (interested / interesting) in the

usual TV shows. He thought the traffic and the people at the shopping mall

were (annoyed / annoying). He decided to go on a long, (relaxing / relaxed)

weekend in the mountains. Out in the country, Eric was (surprised /surprising)

by the beautiful scenery. He was (comforted / comforting) by the clean, fresh

air. He had a great time and took lots of (interested / interesting) pictures.

D Circle the correct adverbs.

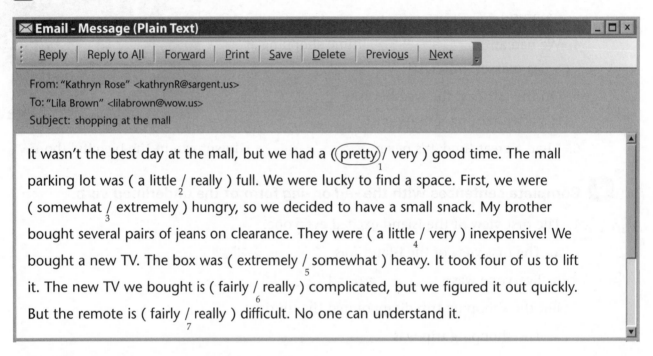

Email - Message (Plain Text)

Reply | Reply to All | Forward | Print | Save | Delete | Previous | Next

From: "Kathryn Rose" <kathrynR@sargent.us>
To: "Lila Brown" <lilabrown@wow.us>
Subject: shopping at the mall

It wasn't the best day at the mall, but we had a ((pretty)/ very) good time. The mall

parking lot was (a little / really) full. We were lucky to find a space. First, we were

(somewhat / extremely) hungry, so we decided to have a small snack. My brother

bought several pairs of jeans on clearance. They were (a little / very) inexpensive! We

bought a new TV. The box was (extremely / somewhat) heavy. It took four of us to lift

it. The new TV we bought is (fairly / really) complicated, but we figured it out quickly.

But the remote is (fairly / really) difficult. No one can understand it.

E 🚀 **Grammar Boost** Complete the sentences. Use your own ideas.

I've always been very interested in computers.

1. I've always been very interested in _____.

2. _____ is the most exciting movie I've ever seen.

3. The students were excited when _____.

4. I think that _____ is very boring.

5. English can be very confusing when _____.

A **Read the conversation. Write the answers to the questions.**
Use complete sentences.

A: Seaside Inn. Kelly speaking. How may I help you?

B: Hello. I'd like to reserve a hotel room with a view.

A: For how many people and on what night?

B: For two people on Friday the 19th.

A: Unfortunately, there are no rooms with a view left
on the 19th.

B: Oh, well. Thanks anyway.

1. What kind of room does the caller want?

    _____

2. Does the caller get a room at the Seaside Inn?

    _____

B **You work at the Seaside Restaurant. Complete the**
conversation below.

> **Need help?**
>
> **Apologies**
> Unfortunately . . .
> I'm sorry, but . . .

You: Seaside Restaurant. _____
                                  your name
            speaking. How may I help you?

Customer: Hello. I'd like to reserve a table by the window.

You: _____
                                 1
Customer: For four people on Friday the 19th at 8:00.

You: _____
                                 2
Customer: Are there any tables available at 9:00?

You: _____
                                 3
Customer: Oh well. Thanks anyway.

C **Complete the sentences. Use *so*, *such*, or *such a*.**

1. The Seaside Restaurant was _____*so*_____ crowded that we couldn't get a table.

2. We went to that Chinese restaurant that had _____ good review in
    the paper.

3. They had _____ good fish that everyone ordered it.

4. It was _____ late by the time we got back that I couldn't call you.

A Read the article.

Online Auctions: A Global Marketplace

Online auctions make it possible for ordinary people to buy and sell things on the Internet. Here's how an auction works. Imagine that you want to sell a chair. You write a description of the chair and take a picture of it. Then you put the picture "up" on an auction website. You also decide on an opening price for the chair—let's say $5.00. Now people can go online and see your chair and all of this information.

Person A sees your chair and likes it, so he or she makes a bid—an offer to buy the chair at a certain price—for example, $10.00. Then Person B sees the chair and also wants to make a bid. This person has to bid more than $10.00, so he or she might bid $15.00. It goes on like this until the time for the auction is over. Each person who makes a bid has to bid more than the previous bidder. You then sell the chair to the highest bidder. If you're lucky, you'll get a good price for your chair.

The largest online auction site, eBay, started in 1995. It now has a membership of more than 100 million people. It is extremely popular all over the world. There are local websites in various countries in Europe, Asia, Australia, and South America. People buy and sell all kinds of things online, from books to cars to houses and many unusual items as well. One woman even wanted to "sell" her husband on eBay! But eBay said, "No! You can't do that."

B Look at A. Mark the sentences T (true) or F (false).

__T__ 1. You don't have to be an official business person to sell things online.

_____ 2. A *bid* is an offer to sell something at a certain price.

_____ 3. In an auction, there is a limited number of bidders.

_____ 4. Millions of people are now buying and selling things on eBay.

_____ 5. You can buy a husband or wife on eBay.

A **Read the catalog.**

Heavy-duty, waterproof flashlight
<u>Long-lasting</u> batteries (150 hours)

Woman's business suit with fitted jacket
Matching blouse also available

Convenient, folding baby stroller
Beautifully (decorated) with your child's
favorite characters

Delicious, naturally flavored fruit bars!
Each box contains 8 individually
packaged bars

Blue jeans, just the right faded look!
Relaxed fit, great-looking

Men's shoes
Designed for comfort

B **Look at A. Complete the tasks.**

1. One adjective ending in -*ing* is underlined. Find three more and underline them.
2. One adjective ending in -*ed* is circled. Find six more and circle them.

LESSON 1 **Vocabulary**

A Look at the flyer. Write the correct words under each picture. Then complete the paragraph. Use the words in the box.

active lifestyle	good nutrition	heredity
~~yearly physicals~~	prenatal care	dental checkups

5 Keys to Good Health

yearly physicals				
1	2	3	4	5

Your _____, or family history, is also an important
 6
part of your health history. It's important to have regular medical screenings
for conditions that are common in your family.

Early detection can save your life!

B Circle the correct words.

1. She has mild but (severe /(chronic)) headaches, two or three every month.

2. The doctor asked if you are (allergic / chronic) to any foods.

3. From your (symptoms / allergies), I would say you probably have a cold.

4. Measles used to be a common childhood (disease / weakness).

5. He's had some (disease / weakness) in that arm since he broke it last year.

A **Read the letter. Complete the paragraphs with the sentences in the box.**

> The doctor suggested a low-salt diet.
>
> She said I should exercise at least three times a week.
>
> ~~I went to the doctor last week for a checkup.~~
>
> Mine is a little high, too.
>
> And I have more energy.

Tuesday, March 28

Dear Gloria,

Thanks for your letter. I'm glad to hear that you had such a good time on your vacation.

Everything's OK here. <u>I went to the doctor last week for a checkup.</u>
                                                                              1
She said I'm in good health, but I have to lose a little weight.

_____ Well, I now walk every morning for 30
                    2
minutes, and so far, I've lost two pounds! _____
                                                              3
You said that your blood pressure is high. I guess high blood pressure runs

in our family. _____ I need to lower it.
                          4
_____ No more salty potato chips for me!
                    5
We're all looking forward to seeing you when you come next month.

Love from your sister,
Teresa

B **Look at A. Write answers to the questions. Use complete sentences.**

1. What did the doctor say about Teresa's weight? <u>She has to lose a little weight.</u>

2. How does Teresa exercise? _____

3. What's the problem with Teresa's blood pressure? _____

4. Why shouldn't Teresa eat potato chips? _____

A Complete the sentences. Use the affirmative or negative forms of the words in parentheses.

1. Debra _____*shouldn't cancel*_____ her doctor's appointment. (should, cancel)

2. Debra and Jon _____ every day. (ought to, exercise)

3. Jon has high blood pressure. He _____ a lot of salty food. (had better, eat)

4. Debra _____ any weight at this time. (should, lose)

5. Debra _____ a lot of rest. (should, get)

6. Jon _____ sugar. (ought to, cut out)

B Unscramble the sentences.

1. blood test / Debra / tomorrow / has a

   *Debra has a blood test tomorrow.*_____

2. nervous / She / shouldn't / the test / feel / about

   _____

3. said that / anything after / she had / not / midnight / better / eat / The doctor

   _____

4. ought to / water before / the test / drink some / She

   _____

5. follow all / She had / instructions carefully / doctor's / of the / better

   _____

6. ought / review / Her doctor / to / the test results / her / with

   _____

C Match the sentences with the advice.

<u>c</u> 1. Sergio works too hard.

_____ 2. One day he got sick at work.

_____ 3. Dr. Ana Garcia examined him.

_____ 4. The doctor gave Sergio some advice.

_____ 5. Sergio's boss, Mr. Ward, also gave him some advice.

a. His co-workers said, "You must go to the hospital."

b. She said, "Sergio, you really ought to take a vacation."

c. His children say, "Dad, you should work fewer hours."

d. He said, "Sergio, you've got to stop working so much overtime!"

e. She said, "I'd better do some tests to see what the problem is."

D Mark the sentences M (mild), S (strong), or SR (stronger).

<u>SR</u> 1. You must go to the hospital.

_____ 2. Sergio, you really ought to take a vacation.

_____ 3. Dad, you should work fewer hours.

_____ 4. Sergio, you've got to stop working so much overtime!

_____ 5. You'd better stay in the hospital for a couple of days.

E **Grammar Boost** Find the error in the underlined part of each sentence. Then rewrite the sentence correctly.

1. <u>I've got wait</u> a long time to see the doctor.

   <u>I've got to wait a long time to see the doctor.</u>

2. You <u>must to take</u> some time off.

   _____

3. You <u>ought go</u> to the pharmacy right away.

   _____

4. You <u>had not better take</u> that medication without a prescription.

   _____

5. He <u>shouldn't to leave</u> the hospital.

   _____

Everyday conversation

A Complete Teresa's part of the conversation. Use the sentences in the box.

> What else do you recommend?
>
> What can I do to lower my blood pressure?
>
> So I should eat a lot of fruits and vegetables, cut back on tea and coffee, and try not to worry.
>
> ~~How's my blood pressure?~~

Doctor: Hi, Teresa. How have you been since your last checkup?

Teresa: I'm a little tired, but I'm OK. <u>How's my blood pressure?</u>
1

Doctor: Your blood pressure is still a little high, but it's not too bad.

Teresa: Oh, dear. _____
2

Doctor: Well, you can eat a lot of fruits and vegetables and cut back on tea and coffee.

Teresa: I see. _____
3

Doctor: You should try not to worry.

Teresa: _____
4

Sounds good, but how am I supposed to stop worrying?

B Complete the sentences. Use the infinitive or gerund form of the verb in parentheses. Check (✓) the sentence that has two possible answers.

_____ 1. When did you decide _____<u>to see</u>_____ the doctor? (see)

_____ 2. How do I know when I need _____ my blood pressure? (check)

_____ 3. The problem is I like _____ salty foods. (eat)

_____ 4. I'll quit _____ overtime. (work)

_____ 5. I have got to avoid _____ coffee or soda. (drink)

C **Real-life math** Read about Teresa. Circle the answer.

When Teresa walks, she uses a pedometer, a machine that counts the steps she takes. She takes 30 steps per 100 feet. There are 5,280 feet in one mile. About how many steps does she take in a mile?

a. 1,600   b. 2,000   c. 2,800

A Read the article.

Chocolate for Your Health

A box of chocolate is always a good present on Valentine's Day, but did you know that chocolate might be good for you? Doctors have studied members of the Kuna Indian tribe to learn how healthy chocolate is. The Kuna live on islands in the Caribbean Sea. They are very healthy. The Kuna almost never have high blood pressure or heart disease, although they eat a lot of salty food. Interestingly, the Kuna diet includes four or five cups a day of a drink made from raw cocoa. (Chocolate is made from the beans of the cocoa plant.) Doctors think this might be the reason for the Kunas' good health.

The healthy ingredients in cocoa are called flavanols. Flavanols help prevent heart disease. Because flavanols have a bitter[1] taste, most chocolate makers remove them. Milk chocolate and white chocolate, for example, have no flavanols. However, high-quality dark chocolate may have enough flavanols to be good for the heart. Of course, if you don't like dark chocolate, you can always reduce stress and get healthier by living on a beautiful Caribbean island!

[1] bitter: with a bad taste, not sweet

B Look at A. Circle *a* or *b*.

1. The Kuna Indians live _____.

   a. in a big city   (b.) on islands

2. Doctors believe that the Kunas' good health might be because of _____.

   a. the salty food they eat   b. the cocoa they drink

3. Flavanols have a _____ taste.

   a. bitter   b. sweet

4. _____ chocolate is healthier for you than white chocolate.

   a. Milk   b. Dark

A Read the form.

HEALTH HISTORY

PLEASE PRINT

Name: Yoon   Ben   Alan

Last name   First name   Middle name

Address: 295 Elm Street   Alto Crest   NM 88345 (505) 555-4362

Street address   City   State/Zip   Phone

Date of birth: 8/26/1962   Place of birth: Utica, New York   Sex:(M)/ F

Month/day/year

Person to notify in an emergency:

Name / relationship: Emma Thomas/sister   Home phone: (505) 555-5430

Personal Physician: Dr. Mark Perez   22 Main St. Suite 203   (505) 555-6897

Name   Address   Phone

Allergies: pet hair, chocolate, aspirin

Have you ever had or do you now have any of the following?

	Yes	No		Yes	No		Yes	No
Bone disease		X	Headaches	X		Overweight (Obesity)	X	
Chickenpox	X		Heart problems		X	Stomach trouble		X
Ear disease		X	High blood pressure	X		Trouble sleeping	X	
Eating problem		X	Lung disease		X	Hospitalization	X	
Eye disease		X	Major injury	X		Other serious illness		X

Please explain all YES answers: I had chickenpox when I was 10. I suffer from chronic headaches (2–3 a month). I take medication for high blood pressure. In 1985, I was in a car accident, and I broke my left arm and leg. I was in the hospital for 2 weeks.

B Look at A. Write short answers to the questions.

1. What is Mr. Yoon's middle name? Alan

2. Where was he born? _____

3. When was he born? _____

4. Who should they call if there's an emergency? _____

5. What disease did Mr. Yoon have as a child? _____

6. What is Mr. Yoon allergic to? _____

7. What does Mr. Yoon take medication for? _____

8. How did Mr. Yoon break his arm and leg? _____

9. Mr. Yoon didn't explain two of his problems in the notes. Which are they?

_____

_____

Get Involved!

A Write the correct words under each picture.

| discuss the issue | develop a plan | implement the plan |
| ~~identify a problem~~ | propose a solution | |

1.

identify a problem

2.

3.

4.

5.

B Match the problems with the departments.

__d__ 1. "There have been a lot of robberies around here."

____ 2. "I need to work, but I have a two-year-old boy."

____ 3. "The streetlight on our corner is broken."

____ 4. "We need a lawyer for a problem in our building."

____ 5. "I need a nurse to care for my mother."

____ 6. "Are there any good summer programs for teens?"

a. Public Works

b. Senior Services

c. Parks & Recreation

d. Public Safety

e. Legal Services

f. Childcare Services

A Complete the letter. Use the sentences in the box.

> There are also many teenagers and older people here who need transportation.
>
> We would like the city to bring a bus line to our area.
>
> Our community is near the intersection of Field and Mason Streets.

Tulia Walters
147 Field Street
Davis, TX 12345
April 27, 2007

Joan Kowalski, Council Member
17 Bernard Circle
Davis, TX 12345

Dear Council Member Kowalski:

P1 I am writing to ask for help with a problem in our community.

_____

There is no bus service in this area.

P2 It is a growing area. Many people need bus service to get to work. _____

_____

P3 _____

You can contact me at 912-555-3490 or at TRWalters@online.met.

Sincerely,
Tulia Walters
Tulia Walters

B Look at A. Answer the questions. Write *P1, P2,* or *P3.*

1. Which paragraph says what the writer wants the city to do? _____

2. Which paragraph introduces the problem? _____

3. Which paragraph explains the problem and gives examples? _____

A **Mark the questions D (direct) or I (indirect).**

_D_ 1. What's the telephone number of the police station?

____ 2. How often do they have loud parties like this?

____ 3. Do you know which apartment the noise is coming from?

____ 4. Why didn't they invite us?

____ 5. Can you tell me when the party started?

B **Rewrite the questions. Change them from direct to indirect questions. Use the words in parentheses.**

1. How many people were there at the party? (Do you know)

   Do you know how many people there were at the party?

2. What are they going to do with all that trash in the parking lot?
   (Can you tell me)

   _____

3. What time did they leave? (Do you have any idea)

   _____

4. What did the landlord say about the party last night? (Do you know)

   _____

5. When are we having a meeting about the problem? (Could you please tell me)

   _____

C Read the flyer. Then read the direct questions. Complete the indirect questions with *if* or *whether*.

> ## What to Do About Barking Dogs
>
> It is illegal for pet owners to allow dogs to bark in the city of Oceanview.
>
> The city charges fines up to $500.00 for barking dogs.
>
> To report a barking dog problem, call the hotline at (915) 555-2500.

1. Does our building have any rules about pets?

   Do you know _if (whether) our building has any rules about pets_?

2. Is it illegal to keep a barking dog?

   Do you know _____?

3. Are there many barking dogs in this neighborhood?

   Do you have any idea _____?

4. Does the city take the dogs away from the owners?

   Can you tell me _____?

5. Is this the right number to call to report the neighbor's barking dog?

   Do you know _____?

D 🚀 Grammar Boost   Study the Grammar note. Then read the direct questions. Complete the indirect questions with *if* or *whether*.

Grammar note: Indirect questions with *will*	
Direct questions	**Indirect questions**
Will he do **it**?	*Can you tell me **if** he **will do** it?*
Will Amy **be** there?	*Do you know **whether** Amy **will be** there?*
When **will** they **come**?	*Do you have any idea **when** they**'ll come**?*

1. Will the new recreation center have a pool?

   Do you know _whether (if) the new recreation center will have a pool_?

2. Will a police officer attend the meeting?

   Can you tell me _____?

3. When will they repair the street near our house?

   Do you know _____?

4. Where will the city put the new traffic light?

   Could you tell me _____?

A Complete the conversation. Use the sentences in the box.

> Do you know if people can speak at the meeting?
>
> I'll be there.
>
> ~~I'm calling because I heard the town is making changes to South Street Park.~~
>
> I'm not sure that a recycling center there is a good idea.
>
> I hear what you're saying.

Sunita: City of Alto Plano. Sunita speaking. May I help you?

Tai: My name is Tai Le. <u>I am calling because I heard the town is making changes</u>
         ₁
         <u>to South Street Park.</u> Is this true?

Sunita: Yes, it is. They're planning to add more parking and a recycling center.

Tai: Hmm… _____
         ₂

Sunita: _____
         ₃
         We've gotten a lot of calls about this. Listen, there's a public hearing on March 7th.

Tai: Great! _____
         ₄

Sunita: Yes, they can. The hearing is from six to nine o'clock in City Hall.

Tai: Thanks. _____
         ₅
         I have a lot of questions.

B Circle the correct words.

1. Tai doesn't know if (are they / (they are)) building a recycling center.

2. She has no idea where (is the meeting / the meeting is).

3. She's not sure when (it starts / does it start).

C **Real-life math** **Read about the vote. Answer the question.**

There were 51 people present at the next town city council meeting. Thirty-two people voted in favor of the recycling center. They needed a 2/3 majority to win.

Did the recycling center pass or not? _____

A Read the article.

What Is a Food Bank?

A food bank is a community organization that collects free food from farmers, restaurants, and grocery stores before it is thrown out. The food bank then delivers the food at low or no cost to people in need.

Food banks give food to childcare centers, senior centers, and homeless shelters. They bring bags of groceries to older people who cannot leave their homes. Food banks also provide emergency food for low-income people. Families with health or employment problems can receive a week's supply of food within hours of filling out a form asking for food help.

The food bank, America's Second Harvest, provides supplies to emergency centers during disasters like earthquakes and hurricanes. In 2005, they sent 1,904 truckloads or 59.8 million pounds of food and water to the victims of Hurricanes Katrina and Rita in the U.S.

Every year, America's Second Harvest distributes 1.8 billion pounds of donated food products. Food banks provide a valuable service to the community and prevent the waste of good food that might otherwise be thrown away.

B Look at A. Mark the sentences T (true), F (false), or NI (no information).

___F__ 1. Food banks buy food from restaurants and grocery stores.

_____ 2. Childcare centers sometimes receive food from food banks.

_____ 3. To get food from a food bank, people have to go to the bank and pick it up.

_____ 4. America's Second Harvest gave 1,904 pounds of food to the victims of Hurricane Katrina.

_____ 5. With food banks, less food is wasted in the U.S.

_____ 6. America's Second Harvest also sends a lot of food to other countries.

A **Read the report of the Public Hearing.**

Minutes[1] for Public Hearing

Alto Plano City Hall

June 7, 6–9 p.m.

Item 1—Public Hearing: Uses of South Street Park

Senior Development Coordinator J. B. Alvarez explained that the Town of Alto Plano proposed new playing fields, parking areas (called "Parking Gardens"), a dog park, and a recycling center for South Street Park. Mr. Ben Yoon described the site design.

Council Member Vance asked why more parking areas were needed.

Mayor Charles asked what the term "Parking Garden" meant. Mr. Seong responded with a description of the design of car-parking areas.

At this point, the meeting was opened to questions from members of the community.

Ms. Tai Le asked why they were planning a recycling center in this location. Mr. Yoon said the community needed a recycling center and that the park offered the necessary space.

Mr. Robert Greene wasn't sure if the new playing fields were a good idea. He expressed concern about increased noise and activity in the park. He also asked if it was possible to use the playing fields for concerts or other performances. The council agreed to explore the idea of using the playing fields for concerts.

The council then agreed to continue the hearing on August 25.

[1]minutes: an official written report of a meeting

B **Look at A. Complete the tasks.**

1. Write four things the town is planning to add to South Street Park.

   <u> new playing fields </u>   _____

   _____   _____

2. One question reported with the word *asked* is underlined in the minutes. Find three more and underline them.

3. Find a sentence that uses the expression *wasn't sure if,* and circle it.

4. Write two things the council agreed to do.

   _____   _____

Vocabulary

A **Write the parts of the web page below. Use the words in the box.**

| cursor | pointer | pull-down menu | search box | scroll bar | ~~URL box~~ |

1. <u>URL box</u>   4. _____

2. _____   5. _____

3. _____   6. _____

B **Look at A. Read the Links column. Write the link each person should click on.**

1. "I want to find the Frequently Asked Questions."   <u>FAQs</u>

2. "Where's the first page of this website?"   _____

3. "I'd like some information about this company."   _____

4. "What's the company's email address or phone number?" _____

5. "Is there anything new I should look at?"   _____

A **Complete the paragraphs. Use the sentences in the box.**

> However, these days, handwritten messages are still important for some things.
>
> Thirty years ago, most personal letters were written by hand.
>
> Now with computers, it's easy to email a letter or send an instant message.

Writing Letters—Then and Now

_____

It took weeks to write and get a reply. Many people didn't like to write letters. Stamps were expensive, especially for overseas mail.

_____

Emailing individual messages doesn't cost anything. Many people write to each other more frequently since it's more convenient and the messages arrive quickly.

_____

Many people prefer sending "real" paper birthday cards or cards for other occasions by regular mail. This is also true of thank-you notes. Most people agree that a handwritten thank-you note means more than an email message.

B **Complete the essay below. Use the notes on the card.**

Essay Notes
1) listen to radio, go to live concerts
2) can buy CDs, DVDs, download music from Internet. Don't need to go to a store
3) live music more exciting, see artists in "real" life, sound better than CD

Listening to Music— Then and Now

One hundred years ago, people didn't have many different ways to listen to music. _____

_____

Now people can get music from many different sources. _____

_____

_____

However, many people still like their music "live." _____

_____

_____

A Match the first part of each question with the correct tag.

_c_ 1. The URL for Skyway was www.skyway.us,   a. are you?

____ 2. Your password isn't "pizza,"   b. was it?

____ 3. You're looking at the home page,   c. wasn't it?

____ 4. We aren't traveling on Friday the 13th,   d. weren't you?

____ 5. You were able to make a reservation,   e. is it?

____ 6. You aren't a landlord,   f. aren't you

____ 7. That Internet connection wasn't fast,   g. are we?

B Complete the conversation. Use tag questions with *be*.

Customer: You're a salesperson, _____*aren't you*_____?
                                              1

Salesman: Yes, I am. How can I help you?

Customer: What's the price of this Bell 560 computer? They're on sale,

_____?
                     2

Salesman: Yes, they are. They're 20 percent off. You weren't interested

in the 750 model, _____?
                                        3

Customer: No, I wasn't, but it *is* nice. They're both equipped with

Internet Star, _____?
                               4

Salesman: Yes they are. Point the cursor at the red star and click.

That was fast, _____?
                           5

Customer: Yes, it certainly was.

C Complete the questions. Use tag questions with *do, does,* or *did*.

1. We don't have to go to the library today, _____ do we _____?

2. You didn't save the assignment on your computer, _____?

3. I sent you Julio's email message, _____?

4. She doesn't know how to take photos with her phone, _____?

5. He didn't take the online English class, _____?

D Write short answers to the questions. Agree or disagree.
Follow the words in parentheses.

1. A: There isn't any more space in our Internet class, is there? (disagree)

   B: _____ Yes, there is _____. There's room for one more person.

2. A: The teacher shows you how to design web pages, doesn't she? (agree)

   B: _____. That's why I'm taking the class.

3. A: We didn't have to sign up for the computer lab, did we? (disagree)

   B: _____. You'd better sign up now before it's too late.

4. A: The assignments are on the website, aren't they? (agree)

   B: _____. Go to the website and click on *homework*.

E 🚀 **Grammar Boost** Study the Grammar note. Then complete
the conversation. Use tag questions with *can* or *will*.

> **Grammar note: Tag questions with *can* and *will***
>
> *You'll come, **won't you**?*   *He can do it, **can't he**?*
> *They won't come, **will they**?*   *We can't do it, **can we**?*

Arturo: You'll come with us on our trip this weekend, _____ won't you _____?
                                                              1

Miguel: What about my research paper? I won't finish it if I go with you,

             _____?
                    2

Arturo: You can use my computer to finish the paper tonight,

             _____?
                    3

Miguel: Yes, but I'll be trying to write. You'll be having fun,

             _____?
                    4

Arturo: No, I have homework, too. We can do it together, _____?
                                                                    5

A **Complete the conversation. Use the sentences in the box.**

> Uh . . . type what?
>
> Can I suggest something?
>
> Type *open a childcare center.*
>
> ~~Have you found out how to set up a childcare center yet?~~
>
> Here's a whole list of sites.
>
> First, turn on the computer and click on the Internet icon.

Angie: <u>Have you found out how to set up a childcare center yet?</u>
1

Rosa: No, not yet. I need some help.

Angie: _____ Why don't you look on the Internet?
2

Rosa: That would be great, but I've never done it before.

Angie: Let's try it together. _____
3

Rosa: What should I type in the search box?

Angie: _____ Then click *Go.*
4

Rosa: _____
5

Angie: *Open a childcare center.*

Rosa: Oh, look. _____ This is great. Thanks!
6

Angie: You're welcome.

B **Match the sentences with the questions.**

_c_ 1. Type *open a childcare center.*   a. Where?

____ 2. Ask Mr. Papadakos to help you.   b. The what?

____ 3. You'd better read the contract carefully.   c. Type what?

____ 4. There are about 50 sites with information.   d. Who?

____ 5. I found the information on the Internet.   e. How many?

A Read the article.

How to Find Useful Websites

What's a search engine?
A search engine is a computer program that searches the Internet for information on certain topics. Each search engine provides a search box for the user to enter keywords, for example, *job search*. The user clicks on the search button, and the search engine looks for pages that contain these words.

How many web pages are listed?
There can be thousands, even millions of web pages for one topic. One search engine generated more than 1,600,000 hits for the phrase *job search*! (In computer language, people refer to each result of a web search as a *hit*.) However, the most popular sites are usually listed on the first few pages.

How do I find the best web page for my topic?
You need to be specific about what you want to find. To look for the words *job search* as a phrase, not as the words *job* and *search* separately, put the phrase in quotation marks, "job search." Then add the type of job you are looking for, for example, *chef*. On the search engine mentioned above, adding the word *chef* reduced the number of hits to a few more than 200,000. To get even fewer, you might add the name of the city where you want work.

B Look at A. Circle *a* or *b*.

1. The words you put in the search box are called ____.

   (a.) keywords   b. a search engine

2. The search for a phrase like *job search* will probably find ____ of pages.

   a. hundreds or thousands   b. thousands or millions

3. To search for a phrase with two or more words, you need to ____.

   a. underline the words   b. put the words in quotation marks

4. To find the information you need, you will probably need to look at ____.

   a. all of the pages   b. only the first two or three pages

5. The results of a web search are often referred to as ____.

   a. hits   b. keywords

A   Read the scene from a TV program. Complete the tag questions.

I Didn't Do It!

Script from *Crime Suspect* Episode 6:
"Robbery on 12th Street"
Scene: Interview room in police station.

Detective 1: You robbed First National Bank,

     _____*didn't you*_____? You and Razor?
     1

Danny: No! No, we didn't. I don't do bank robberies.

Detective 1: Razor does. And you two are really close friends.

Detective 2: You were at the bank yesterday afternoon, _____?
     2

Danny: I was opening an account. That's not a crime, _____?
     3

Detective 1: We can prove you both were involved, _____, Sam?
     4

Detective 2: Yes, we sure can. Razor's fingerprints are all over the back door.

Danny: That doesn't mean I helped him, _____?
     5

Detective 2: Then why did we find this key in your apartment? *[Shows Danny a key.]*

Danny: I've never seen it before.

Detective 1: It's a key to Razor's car, _____?
     6

Danny: No. It's the key to . . .

B   Look at A. Write short answers to the questions.

1. What do the detectives think Danny did? _Robbed the First National Bank_

2. What does Danny say he was doing at the bank? _____

3. What did the detectives find on the back door? _____

4. What do you think? Did Danny help Razor rob the bank? Why?

     _____

How did I do?

Vocabulary

A **Complete the paragraphs. Use the words in the box.**

~~overcome adversity~~	start a business	give back to the community
achieve her goal	had a dream	win a scholarship

David's life hadn't been easy, but his family helped him
<u>overcome adversity</u> and get an education. When he was
       ¹
a teenager, he _____. He wanted to
           ²
own a small restaurant. His father supported this dream and

encouraged him to save money to _____
               ³
in their community.

Goal: business owner

Yan-li always wanted to be a teacher. She needed money to go

to college, so her only chance was to _____.
               ⁴
Everyone helped her to _____. Now she's
           ⁵
able to _____ by helping children.
       ⁶

Goal: teacher

B **Complete the sentences. Circle *a, b,* or *c.***

A person who...

1. is sure of himself is __*c*__.

    a. courageous   b. dedicated   ⓒ confident

2. knows what is possible is ____.

    a. practical   b. confident   c. assertive

3. will try something a little scary is ____.

    a. competent   b. courageous   c. practical

4. works very hard is ____.

    a. dedicated   b. assertive   c. competent

A **Read the prompts. Then mark the sentences T (topic sentence) or E (example).**

1. **Prompt:** Think of one person who has had a positive influence on your life. How did this person help you?

   ____ a. Mr. Sanford, my fifth grade teacher, was one of the most important people in my life.

   ____ b. When I was having problems with math, Mr. Sanford gave me extra help.

2. **Prompt:** Why is it important for successful people to give back to the community?

   ____ a. David Wright started a business in his community, and this provided jobs for many people there.

   ____ b. When successful people give back to the community, they help make the whole community a better place to live.

B **Read the prompt. Complete the essay. Use the sentences from the paragraph boxes. Choose the correct topic sentence for each paragraph.**

Prompt: Describe one positive change in your life recently. How will this change affect your future?

Paragraph 1
Now I am working during the day and studying at night.
Last year I decided to get a degree in hotel management at a local college.
However, my family has been very helpful.
This means that I have less time for my family.
Paragraph 2
After I finish my degree, I'll be able to get a great job.
Having more education will help me in the future.
I'll earn a good salary.

_____

_____

_____

They know I have wanted to do this for a long time. _____

_____

_____

I know that someday I'll be a great hotel manager. _____

A Complete the sentences with the gerund form of the verb in parentheses.

There are two college students who run the front desk at the Valley Recreation Center. Karin knows a lot about ___using___ (use) the computer

1

to register new clients. She works very hard. Instead of _____ (leave)

2

right at five o'clock every day, Karin stays late to plan activities. She cares

about _____ (help) people who have problems. Ricky, the other front

3

desk clerk, is from Mexico. He's the soccer coach. He does a good job of

_____ (coach) the junior soccer team. He's wonderful with people, but

4

he needs to work on _____ (speak) more clearly on the telephone.

5

B Complete the sentences. Use the verbs in parentheses and gerunds.

Hua-li (Holly) Xu works at a flower shop called City Flowers next to

the hospital. Holly ___works on creating___ (work on, create) beautiful

1

flower baskets. She likes her job because she _____

2

(believe in, make) the hospital patients feel better. Holly's boss, Leanne, also

_____ (care about, keep) the customers happy. Leanne is a

3

good boss. She _____ (talk about, help) Holly open a small

4

flower shop of her own. Holly _____ (look forward to, start)

5

her own business.

C Complete the paragraph. Use the words in the box.

nervous about	responsible for	~~proud of~~	excited about

It was Luc's first day as an emergency technician. He felt very

_____proud of_____ being chosen out of ten applicants. Luc
      1

was _____ having this opportunity, but he was
      2

_____ making a mistake. His boss told Luc that he was
      3

_____ driving the ambulance safely. Luc tried his best
      4

to follow directions, and he did a good job on his first day.

D Complete the sentences with gerunds. Use your own ideas.

I'm interested in taking some courses in accounting.

1. I'm interested in _____.

2. I'm excited about _____.

3. I'm nervous about _____.

4. I'm tired of _____.

E 🚀 Grammar Boost   Study the Grammar note. Then rewrite the
    sentences with gerunds.

> **Grammar note: Gerunds with *before, after, when***
>
> Gerunds are often used instead of time clauses with *before, after,*
> and *when.*
>
> | **Time clause** | *After I write an essay, I ask a friend to read it.* |
> |---|---|
> | **Gerund** | *After writing an essay, I ask a friend to read it.* |

1. Before I begin an essay, I make notes about my ideas.

   Before beginning an essay, I make notes about my ideas.

2. When I write the essay, I don't worry about spelling.

   _____

3. After I finish the essay, I check for spelling mistakes.

   _____

4. After he reads my essay, Mr. Bloom usually gives me some good suggestions.

   _____

A **Number the sentences in the correct order. Then use the sentences to complete the conversation.**

____ Yes, you forgot to tell them the patient's blood pressure.

_1_ Luc you've done a great job today driving the ambulance.

____ You need to be sure to give the doctors at the hospital the information they need.

____ Good idea. There's one starting next week.

____ I'll be sure to remember that. Anything else?

____ Thanks. Is there anything I need to work on?

____ Oh, I didn't realize there was a problem with the doctors.

____ Yes, one more thing. I'd recommend taking an advanced training class.

Supervisor: _Luc you've done a great job today driving the ambulance._

Luc: _____

Supervisor: _____

Luc: _____

Supervisor: _____

Luc: _____

Supervisor: _____

Luc: _____

B **Read the sentences. Then write polite requests or suggestions with gerunds. Use the words in parentheses.**

1. Can I recommend something? Take a training class. (I'd recommend)

   I'd recommend taking a training class.

2. Can I suggest something? Call ahead to the hospital. (I would suggest)

   _____

3. Please tell me where I should take this patient. (Would you mind)

   _____

C **Real-life math**   **Read about Luc. Answer the question.**

Luc is certified as a basic EMT (Emergency Medical Technician). To become an intermediate EMT, he needs about 200 more hours of training. If he takes a class that meets every Saturday for 4 hours, how long will it take him to be certified at the intermediate level?

_____ weeks.

A Read the article.

Leticia Walpole: A Success Story

Leticia Walpole was born in Mexico City. Her father did not believe that women should go to college, but with her mother's help, she secretly took college classes in mechanical engineering. At age 21, young Leticia purchased a bus ticket to Tijuana, Mexico, using her grandmother's gold necklace. In the Tijuana bus station, studying a newspaper, she found an ad for a job as a housekeeper. With the help of her employer, she was hired as a supervisor at an American toy company in Mexico. The company president was so impressed with her management skills that he helped her to move to Los Angeles. Arriving in Los Angeles, she was alone and had only $100.00 and a box of clothes. She needed a job, and she also had to learn English.

Within a week, with the help of an American family, Walpole was taking English classes in a community

Leticia Walpole helps out at a recent community event.

college and working three jobs. Soon she applied for a job with the National Guard.[1] They offered her more training in engineering. Later, when the Guard said that its officers had to have a college degree, she returned to college. She earned bachelor's degrees in science, Spanish, and liberal arts.

Now Leticia Walpole gives talks in many organizations and schools in the Hispanic community. She is an example to young people from other countries of someone who overcame obstacles and achieved their dreams.

[1]National Guard: an organization that supports the U.S. military.

B Look at A. Mark the sentences T (true) or F (false).

_F_ 1. Leticia Walpole's father believed women should go to college.

____ 2. Leticia found her first job by reading a newspaper.

____ 3. The American toy company was in Los Angeles.

____ 4. Leticia knew how to speak English when she arrived in the U.S.

____ 5. The National Guard offered Walpole a job in mechanical engineering.

____ 6. Now Leticia uses her experience as an example to help others.

A Holly Xu has just taken a leadership test. How many points does she have? Add them up. Is she a good leader?

TAKE A TEST TO FIND OUT:

Are You a Leader?

	Often (3 pts)	Sometimes (2 pts)	Never (1 pt)
❶ I win awards or scholarships for success at school or the workplace.	☐	☒	☐
❷ When I have difficulty with a task, I ask for suggestions for <u>improving</u> my work.	☒	☐	☐
❸ If a co-worker has difficulty in completing a job, I try to get someone to help.	☒	☐	☐
❹ I'm comfortable when speaking in front of other people.	☐	☒	☐
❺ I'm very good at reading maps.	☒	☐	☐
❻ I enjoy helping others learn new skills.	☒	☐	☐
❼ I'm happier working with others than alone.	☐	☐	☒
❽ I dream about being famous one day.	☐	☐	☒
❾ I'm on time for meetings.	☒	☐	☐
❿ I don't mind going to a restaurant or a movie alone.	☐	☒	☐

TOTAL EACH COLUMN: <u>15</u> _____ _____

TOTAL POINTS: _____

27–30 points	18–26 points	Fewer than 18 points
You are a natural leader. Other people look to you for leadership.	You can be a leader at times. But other times you're happy to follow others.	We can't all be leaders. People who are good followers are very important, too!

B Look at A. Complete the tasks.

1. In item 2 a gerund is underlined. There are seven more gerunds in the test. Find them and underline them.

2. Complete the test for yourself. Are you a leader?

Unit 1 It Takes All Kinds!

Lesson 1 Vocabulary
page 2

A
2. athletic
3. mathematical
4. social
5. artistic
6. quiet
7. musical
8. verbal

B
1. a visual
2. an auditory
3. a kinesthetic

Lesson 2 Real-life writing
page 3

A
2. I don't like to read auto manuals.
3. I like to do activities with other students.
4. At home, I don't watch TV very often.
5. On weekends, I play soccer and exercise.

B–C
If you know your learning style, you will be a better learner. My friend Pietro is a visual learner. When we are studying new words in class, Pietro always asks the teacher to write them on the board. He has to see the word before he can say it. He also draws a lot of pictures in his vocabulary notebook. He says that the pictures help him remember the new words.

Lesson 3 Grammar
page 4

A
2. tell
3. moves
4. doesn't say

B
2. are practicing
3. is interviewing
4. is not/isn't working
5. is/'s taking

C
2. are/'re playing
3. teaches
4. play
5. learn
6. am/'m working

D
2. NA
3. A
4. NA
5. NA
6. A
7. A
8. A

E
2. a
3. a
4. b

F
1. B: looking
2. A: Listen, hear
   B: listening, hear
3. A: see, Look
   B: looking, see

Lesson 4 Everyday conversation
page 6

A
Liang: No, it's not that easy. The grammar is . . .
Satish: Oh, come on! You can speak . . .
Liang: Well, yes, you have a point. I get . . .
Satish: Yeah, pronunciation is hard. Hey, . . .
Liang: Thanks, Satish. Maybe you're . . .

B
2. d
3. e
4. a
5. c

Lesson 5 Real-life reading
page 7

B
2. b
3. a
4. a
5. b

Unit 1 Another look
page 8

A
Answers will vary.

B
Answers will vary.

Unit 2 Keeping Current

Lesson 1 Vocabulary
page 9

A
2. c
3. f
4. d
5. e
6. a

B
2. top story
3. headlines
4. weather forecast
5. traffic report

Lesson 2 Real-life writing
page 10

A
A masked man walked into the Trust Bank in Watford yesterday. He gave the teller, Louise Martin, a bag and told her to fill it with cash. Ms. Martin looked at the robber and said, "No!" The robber looked at her in surprise and said, "Oh, OK." He then turned and ran out of the bank without the money. After the robber left, bank employees called the police. The police searched the neighborhood, but they didn't find the robber.

B
2. She said "No!"
3. They called the police.
4. No, they didn't.

Lesson 3 Grammar
page 11

A
2. was started
3. were told

4. were injured
5. were rescued
6. were taken
B
2. a
3. b
4. b
C
2. Other fires were started by campers in the area.
3. Two firefighters were injured by falling trees.
4. Team members were contacted by cell phone.
D
2. Was the funding for the library approved?
3. Was the old train station damaged?
4. Were the old train cars replaced?
E
2. When was construction on the new station finished?
3. Where was the new station built?
4. Why was the old station replaced?
F
2. Louisa Wright designed the new library.
3. The city council approved the airport improvements.
4. Jeff Young wrote the Red Canyon news story.

Lesson 4 Everyday conversation
page 13

A
2. No, basketball.
3. Well, you know, teenagers need to keep themselves busy.
4. Maybe they can put the courts over there, far away from the building.
5. I think I'll talk to the committee about it.
B
2. himself
3. myself
4. ourselves

Lesson 5 Real-life reading
page 14

B
2. F
3. T

4. F
5. NI

Unit 2 Another look
page 15

A
1. <u>The</u> town of North River <u>was</u> flooded after heavy rains<u>.</u>
B
2. A theft was reported by North River Bank.
3. The local soccer team was defeated by Watford.
4. Highway 80 was closed during the hurricane.
5. A new bridge was opened across the North River.

Unit 3 Going Places

Lesson 1 Vocabulary
page 16

A
2. a
3. b
4. b
5. b
B
2. stuck in traffic
3. lost
4. out of gas

Lesson 2 Real-life writing
page 17

A
(Do you want . . .) A few years ago I was learning Spanish. So, one day I tried to practice with my doctor's receptionist. I asked her, in Spanish, about my next appointment. She said that it was next Friday at *las dos* (two o'clock). However, I understood *las doce*. That means *twelve o'clock*. On Friday, when I arrived for my appointment, I had to wait for two hours!
B
2. The receptionist said, "I'm sorry. Your appointment isn't until two o'clock."
3. I said, "I probably got confused about the time."
4. She said, "I forgot to give you an appointment card."

Lesson 3 Grammar
page 18

A
2. she
3. they
4. they
B
2. she was waiting on Cedar Street.
3. she wanted directions to the college.
4. Maple Street wasn't too far away.
5. it was going to take 20 minutes to fix it.
6. he had to take a different bus.
C
2. told
3. said
4. told
5. told
D
2. Isabel told her husband (that) she was late.
3. Ramon told Sienna (that) he was stuck in traffic.
4. Rosa told her friend (that) the ambulance was coming.
E
2. (that) he needs his extra keys
3. (that) the keys are in the desk

Lesson 4 Everyday conversation
page 20

A
2. How about trying Airport Drive to Highway 24 east?
3. That's a good idea, ma'am.
4. I bet there won't be much traffic.
5. Why don't we try it?
B
Route 1: Time = 22.5 minutes
Route 2: Time = 17 minutes
You can save 5.5 minutes

Lesson 5 Real-life reading
page 21

B
2. a
3. a
4. b

Unit 3 Another look
page 22

A
2. Natalia told Alexi not to turn on the light.
3. Alexi said the neighbors were on vacation. / Alexi told Natalia the neighbors were on vacation.
4. Alexi said he was going out there. / Alexi told Natalia he was going out there.
5. Alexi said he had to call the police. / Alexi told Natalia he had to call the police.
6. Natalia told Alexi to hurry.

Unit 4 Get the Job

Lesson 1 Vocabulary
page 23

A
2. career counselor
3. financial aid
4. training class
5. job listings
6. resource center
B
2. a
3. b

Lesson 2 Real-life writing
page 24

A
2. auto mechanic
3. two years
4. Valley Vocational College
5. three years
6. Gary's Garage
7. available
8. immediately
9. 317-962-2953
10. jbeck@wol.us
B
2. b
3. b

Lesson 3 Grammar
page 25

A
2. had not worked
3. had taken
4. had driven
5. had had
6. had interviewed

B
2. Atim and Malik went to the job fair after they had read a flyer about it.
3. After they had filled out job applications, they were called for interviews.
4. After they had passed their job interviews, they were both offered jobs.
5. J. Stevens Co. had hired 25 new employees before their new office opened in September.
C
2. Why hadn't he taken the training workshop before he started the job?
3. Had he ever had a job before he got this one?
4. Which manager had he spoken to before he arrived for the interview?
5. How long had he waited when they finally called him?
D
2. had already arrived
3. had already completed
4. had already put
5. had already prepared

Lesson 4 Everyday conversation
page 27

A
2. I'd been a cashier and an assistant manager in two restaurants.
3. I took a management training class at the Jade Hotel.
4. Yes, that's the one.
5. Thanks, Mr. Ellis. How about Monday?
B
2. had been
3. found
4. has worked
5. had finished
6. has seen

Lesson 5 Real-life reading
page 28

B
2. a
3. a
4. b

Unit 4 Another Look
page 29

A
2. . . . , his family had just moved to the U.S.
3. . . . , personal computers had not become popular.
4. . . . , he had already started high school.
5. . . . , he had already graduated from high school.
6. . . . , he hadn't started his own business.
B
Answers will vary.

Unit 5 Safe and Sound

Lesson 1 Vocabulary
page 30

A
2. a
3. b
4. e
5. f
6. c
B
2. Be alert
3. Avoid
4. activities
5. report it

Lesson 2 Real-life writing
page 31

A
I. C. Don't use a gas stove for heat.
II. In case of a fire:
II. C. 1. Teach them to dial 911.
III. A. 1. Don't go outside.
III. B. If you are outside:

Lesson 3 Grammar
page 32

A
2. must
3. must not
4. must not
5. must
6. must
B
2. You have to wear gloves.
3. She has to get a new one.
4. He doesn't have to call 911.
5. I don't have to use a map.
6. They have to listen for the warnings.

7. She has to drive slowly.
8. He has to stay inside.

C

2. They didn't have to get batteries for the radio.
3. They didn't have to learn about evacuation routes.
4. They had to bring in all the furniture from the yard.
5. They had to put their bicycles in the garage.

D

2. The manager told Karl (that) he had to remove the boxes from the hallway.
3. Karl said (that) he had to use a ladder for that job.
4. The manager told the employees (that) they had to be careful with flammable liquids.

Lesson 4 Everyday conversation
page 34

A

2. We've got to fix it before dinner.
3. There's a problem with the front door lock.
4. The floor is wet.
5. Anyway, I'll take care of it.
6. The streetlight is broken.

B

2. He should have fixed the stove.
3. She should have told him about the leak in the bathroom.
4. Emilio shouldn't have parked on the street.

Lesson 5 Real-life reading
page 35

B

2. F
3. T
4. T
5. F
6. NI

Unit 5 Another Look
page 36

B

1. make copies
   leave them on desks or tables, or in mailboxes
2. Circle:
   All teachers have to follow these rules.

All work areas and hallways have to be free of unnecessary objects.
3. all injuries
   hazardous conditions
4. Mr. Kaufman should not have lent his keys to a student.

Ms. Franklin should have locked the window before she left the classroom.

Unit 6 Getting Ahead

Lesson 1 Vocabulary
page 37

A

2. make a suggestion
3. ask for clarification
4. give feedback
5. respond to feedback
6. solve a problem

B

2. flexible
3. honest
4. reliable
5. responsible
6. tolerant

Lesson 2 Real-life writing
page 38

A

1. for promotion
2. Moy Wong
3. accounts assistant
4. mail clerk
5. for one year
6. responsible and honest
7. Accounting Basics

B

(Possible answers)
Re: Employee Promotion
I would like to recommend Joena Cardenas for the position of customer service representative. Ms. Cardenas has worked as a sales associate in my department for six months. Ms. Cardenas always goes the extra mile in her work.

   Ms. Cardenas has shown that she wants to learn more about the job. Last month, she took a special training course in People Skills.

   I hope you will consider Ms. Cardenas for this promotion.

Lesson 3 Grammar
page 39

A

2. which (that) are important to her in an employee.
3. who (that) are organized and reliable.
4. who (that) are responsible and independent.
5. which (that) are helpful and not too long.
6. which (that) are short.

B

2. The paychecks were in the envelope that (which) was in your mailbox.
3. The employees congratulated their co-worker who (that) was promoted to manager.
4. The company offers training courses to employees who (that) want to learn new skills.
5. The customer gave the feedback that (which) was shared with the team.
6. Abdul is the new employee who (that) sits next to me.
7. The manager summarized the recommendation that (which) the employees made.
page 40

C

2. who was responsible
   the manager
3. who is in charge of Payroll
   the Human Resources assistant
4. that had the best interpersonal skills
   the team
5. which was held last Tuesday
   at the staff meeting
6. that use the machine
   the employees
7. that speaks several languages
   the job applicant

D

2. d
3. a
4. c
5. f
6. e

Lesson 4 Everyday conversation
page 41

A

2. What should I do?

3. Sure. Who is Cherise?

4. Oh, yeah, I know who you mean. Thanks.

B

Co-worker: Liz

Supervisor: Ramiro

Assistant: Cherise

Owner: Mr. Torval

C

2. Lydia is the customer whose car is at the car wash.

3. Mr. Torval is the owner whose assistant is Cherise.

4. Ramiro is the supervisor whose team does the most work.

Lesson 5 Real-life reading
page 42

B

2. b

3. a

4. b

Unit 6 Another look
page 43

B

(Underline)

who was working in the food department

whose name was Mr. Bernardo

C

2. Jerry, manager

3. Mel Reynolds, man

4. Sonia, cashier

5. Mr. Bernardo, customer

Unit 7 Buy Now, Pay Later

Lesson 1 Vocabulary
page 44

Assets		Debts		Insurance policies	
Item	Value	Loan	Amount	Type	Premium (1 year)
car	$6,000	auto loan	1,300	auto insurance	$900
house	150,000	home loan	105,000	health insurance	2,500
savings	3,500	Q Card	2,400	home insurance	1,400
income	47,000				
TOTAL	$206,500	**TOTAL**	$108,700	**TOTAL**	$4,800

B

2. variable

3. fixed

4. house

5. insurance premiums

6. miscellaneous

Lesson 2 Real-life writing
page 45

A

P3

P2

P1

P2

B

("Neither a borrower, . . .") It means people should never borrow or lend anything.

(Borrowing and . . .) People often borrow too much money, and then they can't pay it back. Borrowing and lending also creates problems between friends. People get angry if a friend doesn't return something they've borrowed.

(It's true . . .) Some things, like a home or a car, are very expensive. Most people could not buy these items if they didn't borrow money.

Lesson 3 Grammar
page 46

A

3. $219.00

4. got

5. would be

6. $159.00

7. 36

8. had

9. would spend

10. $5,000

11. didn't do

12. would be

B

2. If we had car insurance, I could drive the car.

3. If we didn't save money every month, we couldn't take a vacation every year.

4. If he didn't pay the bills on time, he would have to pay late fees.

C

2. would it cost, went would cost

3. would he stay, found would

4. didn't work, would he get would have

5. helped, would he work would

D

2. 'll have to wait

3. find

4. would be

5. did

6. would be

7. wouldn't have to worry

Lesson 4 Everyday conversation
page 48

A

2. Business Mart is 30 miles away.

3. Well, what if we shop there once a month?

4. When do you want to go?

5. How about if we go on Monday afternoon?

B

2. If Business Mart weren't so far away, they would drive there every week.

3. If Jon didn't buy most of their supplies at Business Mart, he wouldn't save money there.

4. If the coffee shop were busy on Mondays, they wouldn't have time to go shopping.

C

c. $90

Lesson 5 Real-life reading
page 49

B

2. A

3. NA

4. A

5. A

Unit 7 Another look
page 50

Answers will vary.

Unit 8 Satisfaction Guaranteed

Lesson 1 Vocabulary
page 51

A

2. flea market

3. as is

4. on clearance

5. online stores

B

2. defective

3. dented

4. stained

5. faded
6. torn

Lesson 2 Real-life writing
page 52

A
P3
P1
P2
P3
B
I received the camera on
March 20, but there are some
problems with the order.

First, the camera is defective.
It doesn't rewind. Second,
the price of the camera was
$299.00, but on the bill I was
charged $350.00.

If you cannot fix the camera,
please send me a new one.
Finally, I would also like a new
bill for the correct amount.

Lesson 3 Grammar
page 53

A
2. excited
3. confused
4. interesting
5. disappointing
6. boring
B
2. a. disappointing
   b. disappointed
3. a. surprised
   b. surprising
4. a. interesting
   b. interested
5. a. confused
   b. confusing
C
2. exciting
3. interested
4. annoying
5. relaxing
6. surprised
7. comforted
8. interesting
D
2. really
3. somewhat
4. very
5. extremely
6. fairly
7. really

E
Answers will vary.

Lesson 4 Everyday conversation
page 55

A
1. A room with a view.
2. No, he/she doesn't.
B
Answers will vary.
1. For how many people and
on what night?
2. I'm sorry, but there are no
tables left on the 19th by the
window.
3. No, I'm afraid we're so
crowded that there aren't any
tables.
C
2. such a
3. such
4. so

Lesson 5 Real-life reading
page 56

B
2. F
3. F
4. T
5. F

Unit 8 Another look
page 57

B
(Underline)
folding, great-looking,
matching
C
(Circle)
faded, relaxed, fitted, flavored,
packaged, designed

Unit 9 Take Care!

Lesson 1 Vocabulary
page 58

A
2. good nutrition
3. dental checkups
4. active lifestyle
5. prenatal care
6. heredity
B
2. allergic
3. symptoms
4. disease
5. weakness

Lesson 2 Real-life writing
page 59

A
2. She said I should exercise at
least three times a week.
3. And I have more energy.
4. Mine is a little high, too.
5. The doctor suggested a low-
salt diet.
B
2. She walks every morning for
30 minutes.
3. It's a little high.
4. The doctor suggested a low-
salt diet.

Lesson 3 Grammar
page 60

A
2. ought to exercise
3. had better not eat
4. shouldn't lose
5. should get
6. ought to cut out
B
2. She shouldn't feel nervous
about the test.
3. The doctor said that she had
better not eat anything after
midnight.
4. She ought to drink some
water before the test.
5. She had better follow all
of the doctor's instructions
carefully.
6. Her doctor ought to review
the test results with her.
C
2. a
3. e
4. b
5. d
D
2. M
3. M
4. SR
5. S
E
2. You must take some time off.
3. You ought to go to the
pharmacy right away.
4. You had better not take
that medication without a
prescription.
5. He shouldn't leave the
hospital.

Lesson 4 Everyday conversation
page 62

A

2. What can I do to lower my blood pressure?
3. What else do you recommend?
4. So I should eat a lot of fruits and vegetables, cut back on tea and coffee, and try not to worry.

B

2. to check
3. to eat (OR eating)
4. working
5. drinking

C

a (1,600)

Lesson 5 Real-life reading
page 63

2. b
3. a
4. b

Unit 9 Another look
page 64

B

2. Utica, New York
3. 8/26/1962
4. Emma Thomas
5. chickenpox
6. pet hair, chocolate, aspirin
7. high blood pressure
8. He was in a car accident
9. He has trouble sleeping and he's overweight.

Unit 10 Get Involved!

Lesson 1 Vocabulary
page 65

2. discuss the issue
3. propose a solution
4. develop a plan
5. implement the plan

B

2. f
3. a
4. e
5. b
6. c

Lesson 2 Real-life writing
page 66

A

Para 1: Our community is . . . .

Para 2: There are also many teenagers . . . .
Para 3: We would like the city . . . .

B

1. P3
2. P1
3. P2

Lesson 3 Grammar
page 67

A

2. D
3. I
4. D
5. I

B

2. Can you tell me what they are going to do with all that trash in the parking lot?
3. Do you have any idea what time they left?
4. Do you know what the landlord said about the party last night?
5. Can you tell me when we were having a meeting about the problem?

C

2. Do you know if/whether it is illegal to keep a barking dog?
3. Do you have any idea if/whether there are many barking dogs in this neighborhood?
4. Can you tell me if/whether the city takes the dogs away from the owners?
5. Do you know if/whether this is the right number to call to report the neighbor's barking dog?

D

2. if/whether a police officer will attend the meeting?
3. when they'll repair the street near our house?
4. where the city will put the new traffic light?

Lesson 4 Everyday conversation
page 69

A

2. I'm not sure that a recycling center there is a good idea.
3. I hear what you're saying.
4. Do you know if people can speak at the meeting?

5. I'll be there.

B

2. the meeting is
3. it starts

C

No, it didn't pass. (A 2/3 majority of 51 is 34. They needed two more votes.)

Lesson 5 Real-life reading
page 70

B

2. T
3. F
4. F
5. NI
6. NI

Unit 10 Another look
page 71

B

1. parking areas, a dog park, a recycling center
2. (Underlined sentences) Mayor Charles asked what the term "Parking Garden" meant. Ms. Tai Le asked why they were planning a recycling center in this location.
He also asked if it was possible to use the playing fields for concerts or other performances.
3. (Circled sentence) Mr. Robert Green wasn't sure if the new playing fields were a good idea.
4. explore the idea of using the playing fields for concerts, continue the hearing on August 25.

Unit 11 Find It on the Net

Lesson 1 Vocabulary
page 72

A

2. cursor
3. search box
4. pointer
5. pull down menu
6. scroll bar

B

2. Home
3. About us
4. Contact us
5. What's new?

Lesson 2 Real-life writing
page 73

A

Para 1: Thirty years ago, most
. . . .

Para 2: Now with computers,
. . . .

Para 3: However, these days,
. . . .

B

(Possible answer)

(One hundred years . . .)
They could listen to music on
the radio or they could go to
live concerts.

(Now people can . . .) They
can buy CDs or DVDs. They
can also download music from
the Internet. They don't even
need to go to a store.

(However, many people . . .)
Live music is more exciting.
You can see the artists in "real"
life. Also the sound is usually
much better than the sound on
a CD.

Lesson 3 Grammar
page 74

A

2. e
3. f
4. g
5. d
6. a
7. b

B

2. aren't they?
3. were you?
4. aren't they?
5. wasn't it?

C

2. did you?
3. didn't I?
4. does she?
5. did he?

D

2. Yes, she does.
3. Yes, we did.
4. Yes, they are.

E

2. will I?
3. can't you?
4. won't you?
5. can't we?

Lesson 4 Everyday conversation
page 76

A

2. Can I suggest something?
3. First, turn on the computer
and click on the Internet icon.
4. Type *open a childcare center.*
5. Uh . . . type what?
6. Here's a whole list of sites.

B

2. d
3. b
4. e
5. a

Lesson 5 Real-life reading
page 77

B

2. b
3. b
4. b
5. a

Unit 11 Another look
page 78

A

2. weren't you
3. is it
4. can't we
5. does it
6. isn't it

B

2. opening a bank account
3. fingerprints
4. answers will vary.

Unit 12 How did I do?

Lesson 1 Vocabulary
page 79

A

2. had a dream
3. start a business
4. win a scholarship
5. achieve her goal
6. give back to the community

B

2. a
3. b
4. a

Lesson 2 Real-life writing
page 80

A

1. a. T   b. E
2. a. E   b. T

B

Last year I decided to get a
degree in hotel management
at a local college. Now I am
working during the day and
studying at night. This means
I have less time for my family.
However, my family has been
very helpful.

Having more education will
help me in the future. After I
finish my degree, I'll be able to
get a great job. I'll earn a good
salary.

Lesson 3 Grammar
page 81

A

2. leaving
3. helping
4. coaching
5. speaking

B

2. believes in making
3. cares about keeping
4. talks about helping
5. looks forward to starting

C

2. excited about
3. nervous about
4. responsible for

D

Answers will vary.

E

2. When writing the essay, I
don't worry about spelling.
3. After finishing the essay, I
check for spelling mistakes.
4. After reading my essay, Mr.
Bloom usually gives me some
good suggestions.

Lesson 4 Everyday conversation
page 83

A

L = Luc, S = Supervisor

L: Thanks. Is there anything I
need to work on?

S: You need to be sure to give
the doctors at the hospital
the information they need.

L: Oh, I didn't realize there was
a problem with the doctors.

S: Yes, you forgot to tell them
the patient's blood pressure.

L: I'll be sure to remember that. Anything else?

S: Yes, one more thing. I'd recommend taking an advanced training class.

L: Good idea. There's one starting next week.

B

2. I would suggest calling ahead to the hospital.

3. Would you mind telling me where I should take this patient?

C

50 weeks (200 / 4 = 50)

Lesson 5 Real-life reading
page 84

B

2. T

3. F

4. F

5. F

6. T

Unit 12 Another look
page 85

A

She has 23 points. Tai Le is sometimes a leader and sometimes not.

B

(Underline)

1. completing, speaking, reading, helping, working, being, going

2. Answers will vary.